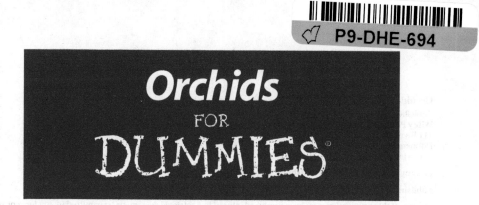

# Orchids
FOR

# DUMMIES

## by Steven A. Frowine and the
## National Gardening Association

WILEY

Wiley Publishing, Inc.

**Orchids For Dummies®**

Published by
**Wiley Publishing, Inc.**
111 River St.
Hoboken, NJ 07030-5774
www.wiley.com

# About the Authors

**Steven A. Frowine** first started growing orchids under lights when he was in high school. Since then, his love and sometimes obsession for orchids has continued to grow. He has tended orchids professionally as a horticulturist, when he worked in Hawaii at the National Tropical Botanical Garden and at Missouri Botanical Garden, where he was Chairman of Indoor Horticulture and managed one of the largest orchid collections in the United States — over 10,000 plants. Steve's greatest pleasure from orchids, though, has been growing them in his own home under lights and in windowsills, which he has done now for over 40 years.

Steve has a B.S. and M.S. in horticulture from Ohio State University and Cornell, respectively. He has had a long and rich career working as a professional horticulturist for premier botanical gardens in the United States and as an executive at top horticultural businesses including W. Atlee Burpee Company, White Flower Farm, and International Gardening Products. Steve is sought out as a lecturer and has delivered hundreds of lectures throughout the country. His presentations are noted for his excellent photography, his knowledge of the subject, and his sense of humor. He has appeared on various national TV shows and writes extensively, authoring many articles for horticultural trade and consumer magazines. His second book, *Fragrant Orchids,* will be released in the fall of 2005.

Steve is now president of his own horticultural consulting firm, where he works with various horticultural companies on marketing and public-relations issues.

The **National Gardening Association** (NGA), founded in 1972, is a national not-for-profit leader in plant-based education. Its mission is to promote home, school, and community gardening as a means to renew and sustain the essential connection between people, plants, and the environment. For more information on the National Gardening Association, visit its Web site at www.garden.org.

# Dedication

To my mother, Janet, and my late father, Samuel, who encouraged me to pursue in my life and work what I loved and believed in.

To my loving wife, Sascha, who shares my passions and tolerates my obsessions.

# Author's Acknowledgments

Many thanks are extended to Glen Decker, who served as the technical editor for this book. It is comforting to have someone with Glen's extensive experience and knowledge pore over my manuscript and lend his constructive, helpful criticism, as well as make sure the information presented rings true. To my Project Editor, Elizabeth Kuball, who greatly helped to mold and shape this book to be the best it could be, and to Tracy Boggier, my Acquisitions Editor, who helped me pitch this book to the folks at Wiley, more thanks.

I am also appreciative to the National Gardening Association, which does admirable good works, and specifically to Larry Sommers and Charlie Nardozzi, of this organization, for giving me the opportunity to produce this book.

The American Orchid Society, *The Orchid Digest,* and the International Phalaenopsis Society deserve a round of applause for the world-class publications they produce and the information they disseminate to the legends of new and veteran orchid lovers. I have made frequent use of all of them for many years.

The orchid community of amateur and professional growers and orchid societies, who inform members and put on orchid shows, get accolades for their dedication and efforts. Many have been immensely helpful to me.

Lastly, I want to thank my wife, Sascha, for her patience in putting up with me pounding away at the keyboard for seemingly countless days, evenings, and weekends, and to my dogs, Ginger and Zoe, who always provided pleasant company and never complained (unless I didn't feed them on time!).

# Publisher's Acknowledgments

We're proud of this book; please send us your comments through our Dummies online registration form located at www.dummies.com/register/.

Some of the people who helped bring this book to market include the following:

*Acquisitions, Editorial, and Media Development*

**Project Editor:** Elizabeth Kuball

**Acquisitions Editor:** Tracy Boggier

**Technical Editor:** Glen Decker

**Editorial Manager:** Michelle Hacker

**Editorial Supervisor:** Carmen Krikorian

**Editorial Assistants:** Courtney Allen, Nadine Bell

**Cover Photos:** © ChromaZone Images/ Index Stock Imagery/PictureQuest

**Cartoons:** Rich Tennant, www.the5thwave.com

*Composition*

**Project Coordinator:** Adrienne Martinez

**Layout and Graphics:** Karl Brandt, Andrea Dahl, Joyce Haughey, Stephanie D. Jumper, Barry Offringa, Jacque Roth, Heather Ryan, Brent Savage, Rashell Smith

**Proofreaders:** Laura Albert, Leeann Harney, Jessica Kramer, TECHBOOKS Production Services

**Indexer:** TECHBOOKS Production Services

---

*Publishing and Editorial for Consumer Dummies*

**Diane Graves Steele,** Vice President and Publisher, Consumer Dummies

**Joyce Pepple,** Acquisitions Director, Consumer Dummies

**Kristin A. Cocks,** Product Development Director, Consumer Dummies

**Michael Spring,** Vice President and Publisher, Travel

**Brice Gosnell,** Associate Publisher, Travel

**Kelly Regan,** Editorial Director, Travel

*Publishing for Technology Dummies*

**Andy Cummings,** Vice President and Publisher, Dummies Technology/General User

*Composition Services*

**Gerry Fahey,** Vice President of Production Services

**Debbie Stailey,** Director of Composition Services

# Contents at a Glance

# Table of Contents

# Introduction

● ● ● ● ● ● ● ● ● ● ● ● ● ● ● ● ● ● ● ● ● ● ● ● ● ● ● ● ● ● ● ● ● ● ● ● ● ● ● ● ● ● ● ● ● ●

*B*elieve it or not, orchids — the most glamorous and spectacular flowering plants in the world, nature's true masterpieces — are easy to grow! You just need to give them what they need. And their requirements are not difficult to meet — adequate light, humidity, water, and ventilation. Sure, there are other nuances, like fertilizing, repotting, insect and disease control, but none of these are daunting. I've been growing and blooming orchids in my home for almost 40 years — mostly not in a greenhouse, but under lights or on the windowsill.

Helping you achieve success with these glorious plants is my pleasurable mission. If you follow the steps I lay out in this book, you *will* grow orchids that thrive. Everything in this book comes from many years of my own trials and errors — not from theories about what *should* happen or what orchids *might* need. Sure, I'm a professional horticulturist, but probably more importantly, I'm a hands-on, sometimes fanatical, home orchid grower. I don't share with you anything in this book that I haven't tried myself or am sure that works.

Years ago, the methods of orchid culture were well-guarded secrets, hoarded by commercial growers and private estate gardeners. That's not the case here. This is a tell-all book where all secrets are revealed. So you can now enter this wonderful world of orchids without fear, knowing that you're armed with the information you need to be successful and enjoy one of the most rewarding and fascinating, lifelong hobbies that you'll ever experience — growing orchids.

## About This Book

This book gives you all you need to know to grow, appreciate, and bloom orchids in your home — in a concise, easy-to-read manner. This family of plants is so humongous that you may be overwhelmed by the prospect of choosing and growing one of your own, so I show you only the groups of orchids that are the easier ones to grow. I also make a point of adding lots of illustrations and photos (most of which were taken by me) to show you what I'm talking about.

I want you to feel comfortable with these dazzling plants and get to know them on a personal basis. Then you'll be eager to discover all their mysteries by slowing down your busy life to savor orchids' inimitable flowers, inhale their sensuous perfumes, and observe the unique construction of their roots and leaves.

# Conventions Used in This Book

Orchid names are in Latin, which is a challenge for most people (except your high school Latin teacher) to pronounce and remember. Don't worry about it. Just get into these names gradually. Take some solace in knowing everyone else is struggling with them, too!

With such a complex group of plants come names and jargon to match. This aspect of orchid growing is what scares most people off. Don't let this happen to you! They're just names and words that scientists have assigned to plants because they had to call them something. Think of orchid names as another language that you can figure out as you go along — with my help. In this book, I make the jargon as simple as possible and explain each term in a way that is easy to understand.

# Foolish Assumptions

In writing this book, I've assumed a few things about you and your experience with orchids. At least one of the following applies to you:

- ✔ You've seen orchid plants in bloom for sale in the garden section of your local home-improvement store or garden center and you've always wanted to give them a try.

- ✔ You purchased your first orchid and are wondering, "Now what?!"

- ✔ You saw orchids at a flower show and you wonder if you can grow these exquisite flowers in your home.

- ✔ You've had some orchids for a few years, but they don't seem to be doing well and you can't get them to bloom again.

- ✔ You've grown some other houseplants successfully and are now ready to move up to orchids.

# How This Book Is Organized

This book is organized into parts, each of which contains several chapters.

## Part I: Welcoming Orchids into Your Life

In this part, I show you how orchids are different from other plants, what makes them so appealing, and where they're found in nature. You get tips on how to select the right orchid for you, which tools you need to grow them, and how you can fully enjoy their beauty in your home.

Chapter 1 tells you what makes an orchid an orchid, where they grow, where they're found, and how they're named. Chapter 2 helps you select the orchid that's just right for you and tells you how to give it basic care for its first days in your home. Chapter 3 gives you a rundown of the tools you'll need to be an amateur orchid grower. Chapter 4 helps you get the most out of displaying your orchid's beauty in your home.

## Part II: The Basics of Orchid Parenthood

This is the nitty-gritty on the basics of orchid care.

Chapter 5 gives you the information you need to provide your orchids with the growing environment that they need to thrive. Chapter 6 addresses the important topics of watering and fertilizing. Chapter 7 eliminates your fears of repotting by giving you the detailed information you need. Chapter 8 guides you through various methods of multiplying the orchids you have. Chapter 9 shows you simple and safe ways to keep your orchids healthy.

## Part III: The Best Orchids for Rookies

Here I introduce you to the most popular and easiest orchid to grow. I've included plenty of pictures so you can see what they actually look like.

Chapter 10 deals with the easiest of all the orchids, the moth orchids. I also introduce you to some of its recommended relatives. Chapter 11 covers the colorful and favorite cattleyas and their relatives. Chapter 12 covers slipper orchids. These are among the easiest to grow with handsome foliage. They have one of the largest groups of ardent admirers. Chapter 13 is about the oncidium group, which is rapidly rising in its popularity because it's easy to grow and because it produces many fantastically patterned flowers. Chapter 14 tells you about more orchid gems that are not quite as common but are worth the search to find.

## Part IV: The Part of Tens

This wouldn't be a *For Dummies* book without a Part of Tens. This is where you can turn when you're short on time but still want a lot of useful information.

Chapter 15 helps you select the easiest orchids to start with. Chapter 16 tells you the ten most common ways orchids are killed and how to prevent these plights. Chapter 17 gives you answers to the ten most common questions asked about orchids and their culture. Chapter 18 informs you about the ten most common reasons that orchids don't bloom.

## Appendix

You may be fortunate enough to be close to an orchid grower or supplier, but if you aren't, don't despair — I list some excellent mail-order providers in this appendix. Some have paper catalogs and others offer their plants online.

Although more home centers and garden centers are carrying orchid supplies, you may have trouble finding some of these materials. For this reason, I include some resources that are dependable.

Orchid societies offer valuable services, from providing places to meet, talk about, and display orchids, to producing excellent publications and sources for information. In the appendix, I also list contacts for the key organizations. They'll lead you, if you're so inclined, to others.

# Icons Used in This Book

I use the following icons throughout the book to point out particularly important information:

When you see this icon, you can be sure to find information that will make you a more successful orchid grower.

This icon points out some common pitfalls you want to steer clear of when growing orchids.

This icon highlights information worth remembering when you're working with your orchids.

Take it or leave it. This icon points out information that may help you win your next game of Trivial Pursuit or convince you that you could be the next *Jeopardy!* champion, but it's not essential to your understanding the topic at hand.

When you see this icon, you can be sure to find a particularly fragrant orchid.

# Where to Go from Here

This book is set up in digestible, stand-alone pieces. Pick out sections that interest you most and read them first. You can bounce around in the book any way you please.

If you already have orchids but are having difficulties growing them, you may want to start out with Part IV. It gives you quick answers to common problems.

Trying to decide which orchid you should start with? Look at Chapters 2 and 15. To get jazzed about orchids, check out the section of color photographs. And if you have an orchid that is in dire need of repotting, skip right to Chapter 7.

# Part I

# Welcoming Orchids into Your Life

The 5th Wave                    By Rich Tennant

"This orchid pollinates by attracting flies with a stinky odor and fuzzy black warts on its petals. Sometimes the flies get confused when Russell's around, but most of the time they're just fine."

# In this part . . .

Growing orchids could change your life — forever! It has for me and many people. No other plant family offers the number and diversity of breathtaking and intriguing flowers that orchids do. When you discover that you can actually grow these exotic plants in your home and that they aren't expensive, your resistance will be lowered and your chances of catching the extremely contagious but wonderful obsession or addiction called the "Orchid Bug" are high.

In England and the rest of Europe in Victorian times, these fabulous plants used to be only for the eyes of royalty or well-heeled aristocrats because of the one-time astronomical prices that they commanded at flower auctions. They were grown in elaborate and costly glasshouses, usually by a staff of professional growers.

How times have changed! Orchids have entered the mainstream. They're now the second most popular pot plant in the world and are gaining quickly on the leader (poinsettia)! Because of new techniques and modern growing methods, award-quality orchids are available to everyone at prices lower than ever before. You can buy an orchid plant in full bloom for less than you would pay for a bouquet of flowers from the florist.

In addition to the orchids of today being less expensive, they're also much easier to grow. Most of them have been bred to be compact and easy to grow and flower in windowsills and under artificial lights. Some bloom more than once a year and others are fragrant. And with thousands of hybrids and new ones being produced all the time, there is an orchid that will strike anyone's and everyone's fancy.

Join me in this part as I introduce you to this marvelous plant family. I show you what makes an orchid an orchid, why you just have to give these exceptional plants a try, and help you make decisions about which orchids are best for you and your growing space. This is going to be a fun journey, so let's begin!

# Chapter 1

# Getting the Lowdown on Orchids

*Y*ou're about to enter the wonderful world of orchids. You're in store for an exciting adventure! This is the largest plant family on our planet with an estimated 30,000 wild types (species) and many more man-made varieties. No other plants can compete with orchids for their power to seduce and bedazzle the most jaded plant lover with their fantastically beautiful flower colors, shapes, and textures, and heady and sensuous perfumes.

## Understanding What Makes an Orchid an Orchid

You can easily tell when a rose is rose, but orchids are quite a bit more complex and varied when it comes to their flower shapes and the construction of their leaves, stems, and roots. In Part III, I give you lots of information on flower, leaf, and stem construction of specific orchids. In this chapter, I talk generalities.

Certainly the flamboyant colors of modern orchid hybrids are a standout and are the primary reason these plants are so treasured. But there are so many different types of orchid flowers, so the question is, "Which one is typical?" There is really no correct answer to this question. Many people think of the cattleya-type orchids (see Chapter 11), while others may picture moth orchids (see Chapter 10).

To get a better idea how orchid flowers are constructed, take a look at a typical cattleya flower and compare it to a more ordinary flower, a tulip (see Figure 1-1). Table 1-1 shows some of the major differences between these two flowers.

So what makes an orchid an orchid? The column. This fused sexual structure located in the middle of the flower is what separates the orchid from all other plants.

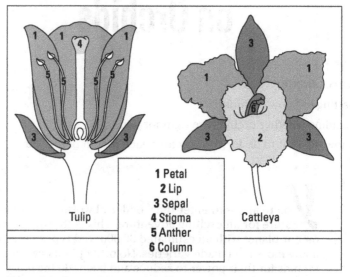

| | |
|---|---|
| **1** Petal | |
| **2** Lip | |
| **3** Sepal | |
| Tulip | **4** Stigma | Cattleya |
| | **5** Anther | |
| | **6** Column | |

**Figure 1-1:** Comparing a cattleya flower with a tulip flower.

## Table 1-1    Differences between Tulip and Orchid Flowers

| Flower Part | Tulip | Orchid |
|---|---|---|
| Petals | The most obvious part of the flower and what makes a tulip look like a tulip. | A very prominent part of the flower but comprises only half of the show. |
| Sepals | Hardly noticeable in the tulip flower, especially after they open. | Very striking in many orchid flowers. Can be as brightly colored as the petals. |
| Lip or labellum | Not found in the tulip. | Usually a very showy part of the orchid flower. Actually a modified petal. |
| Anther and stigma | The two sexual parts of the tulip. The anthers are male reproductive organs and the stigma is the female part. | These separate organs are not found in the orchid; instead, orchids have a column in which the male and female parts are fused. |
| Column | Not found in tulip. | Only found in orchids. |

# Knowing Where Orchids Come From

About 80 percent of orchids are from the tropics in both the New World (Central and South America) and the Old World (Asia and Malaysia). A smattering can be found in North America and Europe.

The ones that grow in your home, though, are all of tropical or semitropical origin. They mostly hail from areas of high rainfall and humidity and enjoy tropical to above-freezing temperatures during the winter.

Orchids are divided into two major categories based on where they grow. Those that are commonly found clinging to branches of trees are called *epiphytes;* those that thrive growing on or in the ground are called *semiterrestrials* and *terrestrials.*

So how can you tell the difference between the two? Many of the terrestrial roots are hairy, like those found in the slipper orchid (see Figure 1-2). Epiphytes have thick roots (called *aerial roots* because they're frequently suspended in the air), which are covered with a silvery material called *velamen,* which can absorb moisture from the air like a sponge (see Figure 1-3).

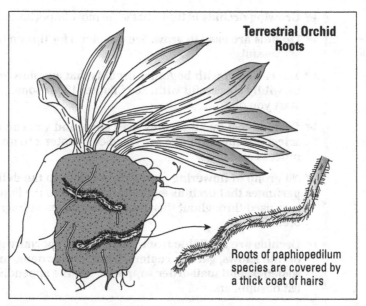

**Terrestrial Orchid Roots**

Roots of paphiopedilum species are covered by a thick coat of hairs

**Figure 1-2:** Terrestrial and semiterrestrial orchids, like most slipper orchids, frequently have hairy roots.

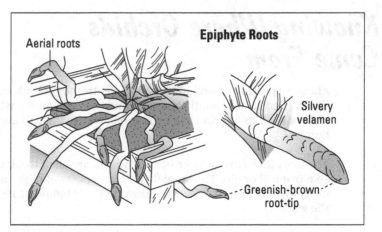

**Figure 1-3:** Epiphytic orchids have thick roots covered with silver velamen.

# Seeing Why You Should Grow Orchids

Growing and studying orchids will provide you the ultimate horticultural experience and pleasure. Here are some key reasons to start growing orchids now:

- ✔ **Growing orchids is fun!** That's the most important motive.

- ✔ **Orchids are easy to grow.** See Chapter 5 for tips on how to be successful.

- ✔ **You can start with beginner orchids that any newcomer can be wildly successful with.** See Chapter 15 for some plants to start you off.

- ✔ **Orchids cost less than they ever have, and you can easily select just the right one for you.** See Chapter 2 to make this process a snap.

- ✔ **No group of flowering plants comes close to the delicious perfumes that orchids emit.** Pay attention to the Fragrance icon used throughout this book to find the most-fragrant orchids.

- ✔ **Orchids are available from "box" stores, specialty growers, orchid shows, garden centers, botanical gardens, orchid societies, and mail-order suppliers.** See the appendix for a list of suppliers.

✔ **Because of the huge diversity of orchids, you'll never tire of them.** You'll always find new ones to try and enjoy. Check out the chapters in Part III for some of the many possibilities.

✔ **You'll meet new friends who are as fanatical about these plants as you are.** See the appendix for lists of orchid societies to join. Their magazines are a marvelous source for information and gorgeous pictures. These are some of the best-quality plant magazines in the world.

✔ **Orchids don't require an expensive greenhouse to grow.** They'll be happy with a windowsill or artificial lights. See Chapter 5 for the skinny on how to grow these orchids to perfection in your home.

✔ **They'll beautify your home and life.** See Chapter 4 for some tips on how to enjoy them to the fullest in your home.

✔ **Orchids can live forever, so as they grow you can divide and multiply them to share with your friends or to trade for other orchids.** See Chapter 8 for more tips on dividing and multiplying your orchids.

# Deciding Which Orchids to Bring into Your Home

Choosing an orchid is an exciting, but sometimes confusing, decision! So many types of orchids, so little space. In this book, I make this process easy for you:

✔ Check out Chapter 2 to walk through some of the steps to take in deciding what orchid will fit in with your home environment and suggestions of where you can scope out and purchase them.

✔ Consider starting your orchid collection with moth orchids. They're the most foolproof of all. See Chapter 10 for details about these.

✔ Next check out slipper orchids, another easy group. See Chapter 12.

✔ Then, if you want to try others, look over Chapter 15 for some of the easiest orchids to grow.

✔ When you're ready to expand or you want more choices, check out all the other orchids in Part III.

# Getting to Know Your Orchids by Name

Probably one of the most intimidating hurdles that the beginning orchid grower faces is the complex names given to orchids. When you realize what an immense group of plants this is, you'll soon come to realize why most orchids are referred to by their Latin name rather than a common name. Actually, very few orchids even have a common name. In this book, I always use the Latin name, because that's the universally accepted name, and I add a common name when there is one.

## Why do I care that an orchid was awarded?

Awarded orchids are the crème de la crème of the orchid world. They've been deemed this distinction by trained, discriminating orchid judges. The American Orchid Society, a nonprofit educational organization that is dedicated to the study of orchids has established the judging criteria. Similar organizations serve the same function in other parts of the world.

At each accredited orchid show, a covey of judges carefully examines orchids that are exceptional. They use Internet connections to check all existing records of the orchids being judged. They look for ones of the same grex or similar parentage to see what has been awarded in the past to serve as a benchmark of excellence. These records will reveal which of their parents have been awarded, what size and number of flowers were on the awarded plants, and so on. These criteria are then used to decide if these specimens are indeed superior to others of this type and whether they're worthy of awards. The three award categories used by the American Orchid Society that you're most likely to encounter are (from highest to lowest):

- ✔ **First Class Certificate (FCC):** This is the coveted highest award that only a handful of orchids (10 or 15!) receive every year.

- ✔ **Award of Merit (AM):** Usually a few hundred orchids win this distinction every year.

- ✔ **Highly Commended Certificate (HCC):** Another few hundred orchids are given this level of award.

Very few orchids make it through this gauntlet. Because of modern cloning techniques (see Chapter 2), you can now obtain these prize winners for your own collection at very reasonable prices. Some types of orchids, like the slippers, are not yet able to be cloned, so in that case, picking out those hybrids with awarded parents is a good idea. *Remember:* It takes the same amount of space to grow a high-quality orchid as it does a poor one, so why not grow the best?

If you struggled through high school Latin classes as I did, you may have thought (and hoped) that this language died with the Romans. Alas, it is alive and well in the natural-science world, and it's the standard language used to name flora and fauna. You'll start to make friends with Latin as its use become more familiar and comfortable to you.

Taking the name a little at a time makes it easier to digest. In the following sections, I show you the names, one word at a time, of a species orchid and then a hybrid.

## Species orchid names

Plants that are sold as they were created by nature, not hybridized by man, are referred to as *species orchids*. They have two names: the genus name, which comes first and is capitalized, and the species name, which comes second and is lowercase. Both names are in Latin, so they're italicized (which is just the way foreign languages are usually treated).

You may see a third part to the name, the botanical variety, after the species name. This is a name given to an orchid that varies somewhat — it could be a larger flower or one with slightly different coloration — from the standard species. It will be preceded by the letters "var." and will be in lowercase and in Latin.

The genus name is much like your last name and the species name is like your first name. In other words, orchid naming is backward to the way you say your own name. If my name were written as an orchid's is, I would be *Frowine steven*.

Here's an example of the name of a species orchid: *Cattleya walkeriana* var. *semialba*. Table 1-2 explains the orchid's name.

| Table 1-2 | The Components of a Species Orchid Name | |
|---|---|---|
| **Part of Name** | **Name** | **Explanation** |
| Genus name | *Cattleya* | The first name of the orchid is the genus and is like your last name. It's always capitalized and in Latin. |
| Species name | *walkeriana* | The second name of the orchid is the species. It's always in lowercase, italicized, and in Latin. |

*(continued)*

## Table 1-2 (continued)

| Part of Name | Name | Explanation |
|---|---|---|
| Botanical variety | var. *semialba* | Sometimes, a third name appears for a species orchid. This is called a botanical variety and means this form of this species has something special about it (for example, flower shape or color) that separates it from the more common form of the species. This name is in lowercase, italicized, and in Latin. |

# Hybrid orchid names

Oh, it would be so simple if naming stopped here, but man got mixed up in all this and started developing *hybrids*. Hybrids result from *crossing* two species (taking the pollen from one orchid to use it to "mate" with another). A marvelous thing happens when two different species of orchids are crossed or mated to each other. Their progeny is usually stronger, easier to grow, and frequently produces larger flowers than either of its parents — which is why hybrids are so desirable and popular.

Here's an example of a hybrid orchid name: *Brassocattleya* Cynthia 'Pink Lady' HCC/AOS. (See the color section for a photograph of this orchid.) Table 1-3 breaks down the name and explains its various parts.

## Table 1-3    The Components of a Hybrid Orchid's Name

| Part of Name | Name | Comments |
|---|---|---|
| Genus | *Brassocattleya* | This genus combines two different genera — *Brassavola* and *Cattleya* — to result in the man-made name of *Brassocattleya*. The name is capitalized, in Latin, italicized, and frequently abbreviated *Bc.* |
| Species | None | This is a hybrid that has several different species in its parentage, so no single one is listed. When an orchid hybrid comes from just one species, the species name will also be listed, lowercase, in italics, and in Latin. |
| Grex | Cynthia | All the resulting progeny from this cross are given a name that's known as a *grex*. Think of this as you and all your siblings having a label. The grex is always written in a language other than Latin, is capitalized, and is not in italics. |

| Part of Name | Name | Comments |
|---|---|---|
| Cultivar (cultivated variety) | 'Pink Lady' | This is a selection from this grex that was deemed, in some way, superior to the other members of the progeny. This name is always in any language other than Latin, is capitalized, is not italicized, and is in single quotes. There are frequently several or more cultivars in a grex. Think of the cultivar as one of your parents' children. You're all labeled with a grex, but the cultivar is you in particular. |
| Award Designation | HCC/AOS | Highly Commended Certificate from the American Orchid Society. (See the nearby sidebar, "Why do I care that an orchid was awarded?" for more information on these designations.) |

Orchid hybridizing can produce plants with quite complex names, especially in some of the very large groups like the cattleyas (see Chapter 11) and the oncidiums (see Chapter 13). In these chapters, I deal with their names in more detail.

You don't have to be an expert in orchid names in order to enjoy and grow orchids. You'll catch onto many other name nuances after you're drawn further into the orchid web. For now, don't worry about them much — they're only names!

Turn to the Cheat Sheet at the front of this book for a list of common genera names that you're likely to run into, along with their abbreviations and pronunciations. Tear out the Cheat Sheet and take it with you when you go shopping for orchids.

# Growing Orchids Easy As One, Two, Three

To be successful in growing orchids, just follow these suggestions:

✔ **Know the environment you have to offer your orchids and match this with the orchids that fit.** See Chapter 5 for more information on your growing environment.

✔ **If necessary, modify your growing area to help your orchids perform to their best.** Check out Chapter 5 for information on how to do this.

For the most common questions and problems, check out Part IV.

Beyond choosing the right orchid for your environment, you have to pay attention to the time of the year to know what your orchid needs. In the following sections, I give you a rundown of the year, month by month. *Note:* You can't be too exact with the timing of this care schedule, because the United States is a vast country with climates from the cold north country to semitropics.

## *January*

This is a period of cold, short days and low light, so orchids don't grow much in such times. Fortunately, many moth orchids, slipper orchids, and some other cattleyas and their relatives will be budding up getting ready to show off their splendiferous blooms very soon.

- ✔ For orchids such as some of the dendrobiums, cattleya species, and deciduous orchids, like the catasetums, this is a time of rest, so you'll want to reduce your watering.

- ✔ Keep the humidity high with good air movement.

- ✔ If you are using well water, warm it up to room temperature before using it on your orchid plants. Ice-cold water can cause forming buds to drop and may stunt new growth.

- ✔ Don't put your orchids too close to the windowpanes or the leaves could be damaged by the cold.

- ✔ Apply very little fertilizer. The orchids won't need it.

## *February*

This is another dark month, but the days will be getting longer and brighter, which should cause an increase in growth.

- ✔ Toward the end of this month, increased light may mean you have to be careful with your orchids that require less light, like the slippers and moth orchids, so they don't get burned.

- ✔ More of your orchids will be showing buds and some, especially some of the moth orchids and some of the oncidiums, should be blooming.

- ✔ Don't overcrowd your plants — make sure they receive as much light as possible.

- ✔ Provide good air circulation to prevent disease problems.

- ✔ Stake your cymbidiums, which should be spiking now.

✔ Don't forget to keep your miltonias and miltoniopsis damp.

✔ If you're growing under lights, take note of when you last changed your bulbs. Fluorescent lamps can lose up to 40 percent of their light output after several months of use. Because new growth is starting on orchids, this is a good time to change the lamps so the plants will receive the most light possible.

✔ Apply very little fertilizer during this month.

## *March*

Finally, signs of spring with longer and brighter days.

✔ Be careful that the increased light doesn't heat up too much in your greenhouse or windowsill. Apply shading if necessary.

✔ The increased light and warmth of this month will mean an acceleration of growth. Sprouting new roots should be more evident.

✔ This is the beginning of the show for many orchids. Many cattleyas, moth orchids, slipper orchids, and oncidiums will be starting to bloom.

✔ As the days get brighter and warmer, you can resume your regular fertilizing schedule.

✔ This month and next are prime times to check out orchid shows in your area.

## *April*

In April, many orchids will be in glorious flower.

✔ You'll probably have to increase the frequency of your watering because of the new plant growth.

✔ As soon as you see new roots emerging in cattleyas, this is the time to repot. Do it before the roots grow a few inches (5 cm) long.

✔ Many other orchids showing new growth can also be repotted at this time.

✔ Be on the lookout for bugs. The warmer temperatures cause them to hatch out.

✔ Dormant orchids should be showing new growth now so you can resume your regular watering schedule.

- ✔ If you didn't apply shading on your greenhouse last month, it may be needed now.

- ✔ A gauze curtain may be needed to soften the light for orchids growing in a south window.

- ✔ Check out orchid shows in your area.

## May

Growth will continue at full speed this month. This is another prime month for orchid flowering.

- ✔ More frequent watering and fertilizing will be called for.

- ✔ If you're in a northern climate, move some plants to a shaded, protected spot outdoors by the end of this month, but be careful not to do this too quickly. Orchids that prefer it warm, like moth orchids, don't appreciate being too chilled at night, not below around 65°F (18°C).

- ✔ Increase your ventilation to remove excess hot air and prevent fungal disease spotting on the flowers.

- ✔ This is usually an opportune time to repot most of your slipper orchids because they should be in active growth now. Also, repot moth orchids and their vandaceous relatives. Attend to this right after they've flowered.

- ✔ Continue your fertilizing program to strengthen new growth.

## June, July, and August

Temperatures are starting to heat up now. Some orchids, like a few of the summer blooming hybrid cattleyas, oncidiums, and slipper orchids, will be in flower.

- ✔ Be sure your windowsill or greenhouse doesn't get too hot. Consider moving the orchids you have in the south window to the east window, where they'll have reduced light and heat.

- ✔ For orchids growing under lights, make sure your growing area gets plenty of ventilation, because it could be getting very warm now under the lights. If you have trouble keeping the temperatures low enough, consider summering your orchids outside in a shaded and protected spot. They'll enjoy the vacation.

- ✔ This is also a prime time for insect problems. If it gets hot and dry, be on the lookout for mites. If it's wet, slugs and snails will be a plague. Aphids and scale can show up anytime. If you need to spray, do it in the morning when it is cool and be sure the orchids are well watered before you spray.

✔ The orchids should now be responding to your earlier repotting efforts with new root growth.

✔ Repot miltonias. *Remember:* They like to be pot-bound, so don't put them in too large of a pot.

## *September*

Cool evenings and shorter days are signs of the change of season. Many of the hybrid vandas will be at their blooming peak this month. Buds will be showing up for the fall-blooming cattleyas, oncidiums, dendrobiums, angraecums, and moth orchids and slipper orchids.

✔ If you're in a cold climate, this is the month to bring indoors any plants that have been summering outside. Before doing this, check them closely for pests. If spraying is called for, doing so is much easier while the plants are outdoors.

✔ These cooler nights are very beneficial for setting flower buds and spikes.

✔ Start cutting back on the frequency of watering deciduous orchids like catasetums (which will have yellowing foliage at this time of year).

✔ This is the time to remove shade on the greenhouse in most parts of the country.

✔ Move orchids that require a lot of light from the east window back to the southern exposure.

## *October*

Some cattleya species and their relatives and hybrids will be in bloom now. So will some moth orchid species and hybrids and oncidiums.

✔ As days continue to shorten and the angle of light gets lower in the sky, position the orchids in your windowsill and greenhouse so that they capture the most light.

✔ For greenhouses and windowsills, be sure your glass or glazing surface is clean. This can make a real difference in light transmission.

✔ Growth will start to slow on many orchids from lower temperatures and light, so reduce watering and fertilizing accordingly.

✔ Get ready for winter. Insulate your greenhouse. Get a standby emergency propane heater.

## November and December

Flowering spikes will be showing up on some moth orchids, slippers, and oncidiums. Some of the nobile-type dendrobiums will be starting to show buds. Low light, short days, and cold temperatures bring most orchid growth to a stop or at least a crawl. You'll see more growth on plants grown under lights than in a greenhouse or on a windowsill because of the additional light that can be provided.

✔ For cold parts of the country, November is the last month to safely purchase mail-order plants before it gets so cold that there will be a higher risk chance for freeze damage in transit. This a great time to visit orchid nurseries to pick out holiday presents for your orchid growing friends (or yourself!).

✔ Put orchids that require more light, like vandas, in a bright window, close to the lights, or high in the greenhouse to expose them to as much light as possible.

✔ Water in the early part of the day to ensure that there is no standing moisture on the leaves. In cold, damp weather, especially, such moisture can cause disease outbreaks.

# Chapter 2

# Choosing the Right Orchid for You

*O*ne of the main reasons some people fail with orchids is that they simply choose the wrong ones. Considering that there are thousands of different kinds of orchids, it's easy to see how people may not know which one to buy. To be successful, you need to choose a dependable supplier, healthy plants, and the type of orchid that fits your growing area. In this chapter, I walk you through the important questions to ask yourself and your supplier so you end up with the orchid that will be just right in your growing spot.

## Figuring Out Where to Shop

Finding orchid suppliers used to be difficult, unless you were lucky enough to live in a very warm area, like Southern California or Florida. Nowadays, because orchids have skyrocketed in popularity, you can find them for sale in myriad places. In the following sections, I fill you in on your supplier options.

### Specialist orchid growers or suppliers

An orchid specialist is always my first choice when I'm buying orchids. Reputable suppliers in this category have been selling orchids for many years, before it was the chic thing to do. Almost all of them are orchid fanatics whose hobby grew totally out of control — so they were forced to either stop buying more orchids or start up a business. They know *everything* about their plants — where they came from, their attributes, and how to grow them. They almost always have the largest selection and cater to both the beginner and sophisticated, experienced growers. They love to help other people discover the pleasure of growing orchids and are full of helpful information.

The only disadvantage of specialist growers or suppliers is that you may not have one near where you live. Of course, that doesn't have to be a deterrent. It just means you'll need to do some planning and search out these growers so you can take your own orchid-buying safari!

Turn to the appendix for a short list of some of my favorite specialist orchid growers and suppliers.

## Your local garden center

Having a local orchid source is very convenient both for buying the plants and for information on growing. Today, garden centers offer more unusual and more interesting plants than ever before — and orchids are among these. The types of orchids they offer varies greatly from one garden center to the next.

Look for a garden center that specializes in tropical plants and houseplants. Unless the garden center is noted for its orchid offerings, the selection will probably be limited. Search out the types mentioned in this book, especially the moth and slipper orchids.

## Orchid shows

At orchid shows, you'll find dazzling displays of a broad range of gorgeous orchids. Be prepared to be wowed! Vendors of orchids are a regular feature of orchid shows, so they're a great place to shop. To find an orchid show in your area, check out the various orchid magazines or search their Web sites (see the appendix).

## Online orchid suppliers

You can buy a fine selection of orchids without ever leaving your home. Most orchid suppliers now have Web sites, and some of the sites are very detailed and informative.

To get started, check out the Orchid Marketplace at http://orchid web.org/marketplace.html and Orchid Mall at www.orchidmall.com. Each of these sites provides many links to various orchid-grower Web sites. If you already know what types of orchids you want, you can use a search engine (such as Yahoo! or Google) to search for them by type or name.

If you use the Latin name when searching for plants on the Web, not the common name, you'll get many more hits. In other words, instead of searching for "moth orchids," search using its Latin name, *Phalaenopsis*. Check out www.chebucto.ns.ca/recreation/ orchidcongress/engname.html for lists of the Latin names with their English common names.

## Home centers and discount stores

Because orchids have had such a meteoric rise in popularity, home centers and discount stores now frequently stock a limited selection of them. The good news: They usually carry the orchids that are easy to grow. The bad news: Getting information at these stores is difficult. But if you're shopping for your first, inexpensive orchid, and if you don't have easy access to a garden center or orchid grower, these are good places to start.

When shopping for plants at home centers and discount stores, find out what day of the week their weekly shipments come in. That's the day you want to be there to get the best quality and selection.

# Considering Your Environment

When you go to shop for orchids, you can very easily get carried away! The excitement of the moment can completely win over rational plant selection. Few beginning orchid growers take the time to consider their environment *before* they buy. Unfortunately, if you do this, you may end up bringing home a gorgeous orchid that's completely wrong for you.

If possible, always choose an orchid that comes close to fitting your growing area. Even though in Part II of this book I give you pointers on how to modify your growing area to make it more suitable for orchid growth, you can only modify your environment so much. For instance, an orchid that is commonly found growing in full sun in Hawaii probably won't take well to a windowsill during the winter in low-light areas like New England. And an orchid from the cloud forest that is drenched with almost constant rainfall and very high humidity probably won't be happy and bloom in the hot dry air of Arizona.

In the following sections, I help you assess your environment so you can be confident that you'll pick out a stunning orchid that is right for you and that will thrive where you live.

## Taking temperature readings

Before you bring home an orchid, you need to consider the average daytime and nighttime temperatures in summer and winter where you live.

To determine high and low temperatures indoors get a maximum/minimum thermometer that records this information and place it in your growing area (see Chapter 3).

For an idea of what your minimum temperatures are outdoors where you live, check out the USDA hardiness map at www.usna.usda.gov/Hardzone/ushzmap.html. If you're a weather nut like I am, you can use a recording weather station that reads the maximum and minimum temperature, humidity, wind speed, rainfall, and barometric pressure every hour and stores this information so it can be charted. Mine has remote sensors and a wireless connection to my computer.

A broad selection of temperature and weather recording instruments are available from the orchid-supplies dealers listed in the appendix.

When you've determined the average summer and winter temperatures in your area, turn to Table 2-1, which lists some of the most common types of orchids by temperature requirements. Notice that some orchids are adaptable enough to fit into more than one temperature range.

When orchid publications refer to *temperature preferences,* they always mean the evening temperature. The daytime temperature is usually about 15°F (9.5°C) higher than the evening temperature.

| Table 2-1 | Orchid Temperature Preferences |
|---|---|
| *Temperature (Nighttime Minimum)* | *Genus* |
| Cool (45°F–55°F/7.2°C–12.8°C) | Cymbidium<br>Dendrobium<br>Odontoglossum |
| Cool (45°F–55°F/7.2°C–12.8°C) to Intermediate (55°F–60°F/12.8°C–15.6°C) | Cymbidium<br>Dendrobium<br>Encyclia<br>Masdevallia<br>Miltoniopsis<br>Zygopetalum |

| Temperature (Nighttime Minimum) | Genus |
| --- | --- |
| Intermediate (55°F–60°F/12.8°C–15.6°C) | Aerangis |
| | Cattleya and hybrids |
| | Cymbidium |
| | Dendrobium |
| | Encyclia |
| | Epidendrum |
| | Laelia |
| | Maxillaria |
| | Miltonia |
| | Oncidium |
| | Paphiopedilum |
| | Phragmipedium |
| | Vanda |
| | Zygopetalum |
| Intermediate (55°F–60°F/12.8°C–15.6°C) to Warm (65°F/18.3°C or higher) | Aerangis |
| | Amesiella |
| | Angraecum |
| | Ascofinetia |
| | Brassavola |
| | Cattleya |
| | Dendrobium |
| | Encyclia |
| | Epidendrum |
| | Neofinetia |
| | Neostylis |
| | Oncidium |
| | Rhynchostylis |
| | Vanda |
| | Vascostylis |
| Warm (65°F/18.3°C or higher) | Angraecum |
| | Phalaenopsis |
| | Vanda |

## Measuring your light intensity

Just as important as temperature is the amount of light your orchid will get. Orchids that thrive in high light need several hours of direct sunlight (preferably in the morning to early afternoon), while those that thrive in lower light will perform with less direct and more diffused light in a windowsill or under lights. See Chapter 5 for more details.

Will you be growing the plants under artificial lights? Most light setups consist of multiple florescent lamps and can provide adequate illumination for medium- to lower-light orchids. High-intensity-discharge lamps are capable of much more light output but can be expensive to operate and generate quite a bit of heat. For more details, see Chapter 5.

How bright is your light? Figure 2-1 illustrates a simple yet effective and reasonably accurate method for determining the intensity of your light.

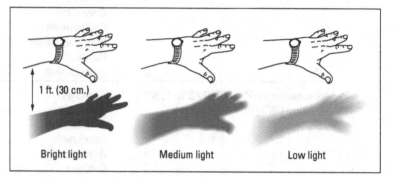

Bright light      Medium light      Low light

**Figure 2-1:** The shadow test is a simple and reasonably accurate way to measure light intensity.

After you determine your light levels, turn to the following sections, which list orchids by the amount of light they need. Remember to keep in mind temperature (see the preceding section).

### Bright light

The following orchids require a bright greenhouse, a very bright south-facing window, or *very-high-output (VHO) fluorescent lamps* (which require specialized ballasts to operate) or metal halide lamps:

- Angraecum
- Some varieties of Cymbidium
- Some varieties of Dendrobium
- Vanda

### Medium light

The following orchids need a shaded greenhouse, an east-facing window, or a four-tube 40-watt florescent light fixture:

✔ Amesiella

✔ Ascocenda

✔ Ascocentrum

✔ Ascofinetia

✔ Brassavola

✔ Brassia

✔ Cattleya and hybrids

✔ Some varieties of Cymbidium

✔ Some varieties of Dendrobium

✔ Epidendrum

✔ Laelia

✔ Leptotes

✔ Masdevallia

✔ Miltonia

✔ Miltoniopsis

✔ Neofinetia

✔ Neostylis

✔ Odontoglossum

✔ Oncidium

✔ Paphiopedilum (strap-leaf multiflorals)

✔ Phragmipedium

✔ Rhynchostylis

✔ Zygopetalum

## Low light

The following orchids do well with a low level of light, easily attainable with two 40-watt florescent lamps or on an east-facing windowsill:

✔ Paphiopedilum (not including strap-leaf multiflorals)

✔ Phalaenopsis

✔ All orchid seedlings

## Other questions to ask yourself

In addition to considering temperature and light, you want to ask yourself the following questions:

✔ **Does the growing area have moist (humid) air, or is the air very dry?** If it is already humid (50 percent or greater), it's perfect. If not, your orchids will be happier with moister air. See Chapter 5.

✔ **How much space do you have to grow orchids?** If you have plenty of head room, you can grow some of the taller orchids, like cane dendrobiums and full-size cattleyas. If space is at a premium, search out very compact or miniature growers. Part III gives you plenty of choices for plants of all sizes.

✔ **When do you want your orchids to bloom?** Spring, summer, fall, or winter? In the evening or during the day? Armed with this information, you can pick those orchids that will be in bloom in the season and time of day of your choice.

✔ **Do you have air circulation in the growing area?** Most homes have adequate air circulation, but if your orchids are going to be located in the basement or some other spot where the air is stagnant, you'll want to consider a fan of some type to provide them with fresh air. See the ventilation section in Chapter 5 for more information.

When you're armed with this information, you'll be better prepared to choose an orchid that will thrive.

# Knowing What to Look for in an Orchid

After you consider your environment, you're ready to go shopping. You have an idea of which types of orchids will work best where you'll be growing them, and now you just need to look at a few things such as the plant's health and age. I fill you in on these factors in the following sections.

## Choosing a healthy plant

Picking out a healthy orchid plant is essential. Even in the best of circumstances, the orchid that you bring home will have to adapt to changes in its environment. A strong, robust plant has a much better chance of surviving this ordeal than a weak plant does.

Here's a checklist of things to look for when you select an orchid:

✔ **Look carefully at the leaves.** They should be stiff, not shriveled or dehydrated. They should also have a healthy green color. Brown or black spots on leaves could mean disease, or they could be harmless; if you find spots, ask the grower about them.

✔ **Look for any signs of insects.** Most insects hang out on the new young growth, on the flower buds of the plant, or on the undersides of the leaves. Also check under the pot for snails or slugs.

✔ **Examine the exposed roots on top of the potting material.** The roots should be firm and light colored, not black, soft, and mushy.

✔ **Watch out for plants infested with oxalis (which looks like clover).** Oxalis is a pesky weed that is difficult to get rid of after it's established. It will not directly harm the orchids, but it can harbor insects and is a cosmetic distraction.

Make sure the plants are labeled. Labels will be important to you later if you want to look up information on growing your particular type of orchid.

Be sure to ask the grower about the temperature, light, and humidity requirements of the orchid you're considering. Check out its ultimate size. Then match this information with what you know about your orchid growing area.

## Deciding between a blooming plant and a young plant

When you buy a mature, blooming plant, you get to see exactly what the flower of this orchid is like. Because many orchid flowers can last quite a while, you'll be able to enjoy this orchid for weeks after you bring it home. The biggest disadvantage of blooming plants is that they're usually the most expensive, because they're in the highest demand.

Younger plants — ones that are months or even years away from blooming — are much less expensive than their mature counterparts. The joy in choosing these plants is anticipating when they'll bloom and what they may look like.

If you're a beginner, I recommend that you buy mature plants with buds or flowers. Waiting for immature plants to bloom is something you may enjoy after you have a small collection of the mature ones.

## Choosing seed-grown orchids or orchid clones

Very few orchids sold today have been collected from the wild. Instead, they've been grown from seed. The flower color, flower size, and growth habits of these seed-grown plants vary. Seed-grown plants are generally very reasonably priced.

*Cloned* orchids, also referred to as *meristemmed* or *mericloned* orchids, are orchids that have been multiplied from single cells, usually from a plant of very high quality, in a flask, which is a type of laboratory bottle. The result is that they're all identical.

The advantage of purchasing a cloned orchid is that you can depend on the orchid that you buy being exactly like its parent, which is frequently an award winner. In general, these clones are a bit more expensive than the others, but they're usually worth it.

# Caring for Your New Orchid

Adding new orchids to your plant collection is exciting, but this is also a time for caution. Even though you may have been very careful in the selection process, your orchid still may be harboring insect eggs that may hatch, or it may have a disease problem that you didn't notice before.

So, to be on the safe side, keep your new plant isolated from all your other plants for at least two to three weeks — enough time to see if any insects appear or a disease shows up. If you need to treat your new plant, doing so will be easier when it's separated from your other plants.

To identify pests and their safest treatment, see Chapter 9.

# Chapter 3

# Having the Right Tools on Hand

• • • • • • • • • • • • • • • • • • • • • • • • • • • • • • • • • • • • • • • • • •

• • • • • • • • • • • • • • • • • • • • • • • • • • • • • • • • • • • • • • • • • •

*E*very hobby has its tools. And just as you need the right saws and sanders if you're building a cabinet, you need the right tools for growing orchids. The amount of tools you need will depend on how serious you are about orchids and haw many of them you have to care for. In this chapter, I fill you in on the tools I use.

## Cutting and Pruning Tools

You'll probably use your cutting and pruning tools more than any others. Orchids always have a leaf that needs to be trimmed or a dead or diseased stem that needs to be cut off. These tools are also used in the repotting process (see Chapter 7). Figure 3-1 shows the kinds of tools covered in the following sections.

### Pruners

You'll need different types of pruning tools, depending on the thickness of the plant part you're removing.

#### Hand pruners

You'll use hand pruners to cut thick creeping stems. There are basically two types of hand pruners. An *anvil type* of hand pruner has a flat cutting blade and can mash the stem tissue (which isn't what you want). I much prefer the other type of hand pruner — the *bypass type,* which has a curved blade (refer to Figure 3-1). It makes cleaner and closer cuts.

### Scissors

All scissors are not created equal. I prefer those that are designed for bonsai or flower arranging (like the scissors shown in Figure 3-1). They're extremely sharp and have large, comfortable vinyl hand grips. Some are made of high-carbon steel that hold an edge for a long time. Others are constructed of stainless steel and offer the advantage of not rusting. The smaller scissors are really handy for finesse work, like removing spent flower spikes as close as possible to the foliage and trimming delicate leaves. The heavier ones are ideal for cutting thick stems.

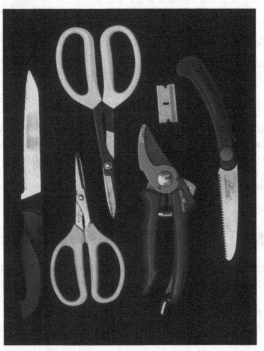

**Figure 3-1:** Cutting tools — from left to right: thin knife, two pairs of scissors, bypass hand pruners, single-edge razor blade, and folding pruning saw.

## Knives and blades

Knives and blades can come in very handy, but choosing the right type is important. In the following sections, I guide you through the types available.

### Knives

Knives are used most often to circle the inside of the pot to remove the plant when its roots are packed into its container, especially with clay pots. (You can usually cut plastic pots with sharp scissors along the length of the pot to remove the plant.) A very-thin-bladed knife, like the type used for filleting fish (refer to Figure 3-1), is very handy because it's easier to maneuver in tight spaces.

### Razor blades

To be on the safe side, always use the single-edge type of razor blade (refer to Figure 3-1). They're perfect for making very precise cuts when trimming edges of leaves or cutting apart divisions of plants. Another great feature of these is that they're so inexpensive that you can throw them away after you're done. Disposing of used razor blades also prevents spreading disease to other plants and saves you the hassle of sterilizing them.

### Hand pruning saw

Using a hand pruning saw is bringing out the big gun. This tool is most useful to cut very thick creeping stems when dividing plants. You can also use them to score the roots when they're very tightly packed together or to cut away a very thick plastic pot when you're transplanting or repotting an orchid.

You can find various different types of these saws, but the ones that are compact and folding are most handy. I find a small bladed and fine-toothed type often used for cutting bamboo especially useful (refer to Figure 3-1).

# Potting Tools and Supplies

The tools and supplies in this section make the potting process easier. For specific potting techniques and guidelines, check out Chapter 7.

## Potting tools

Potting is a combination of force and finesse. These tools make the process easier and more effective.

### Hammers

Regular steel-clawed hammers can be useful for breaking clay pots containing overgrown plants that can't be removed any other way. But for most purposes, a rubber mallet (see Figure 3-2) comes in more handy. It's used frequently to pound in stakes or clamps that hold newly transplanted or divided orchids in their pots.

### Dibbles and planting sticks

Getting the potting material to settle in around the roots of the orchids is important because large air spaces can cause the orchid roots to dry out or not form properly. Dibbles (refer to Figure 3-2) and planting sticks are used to push the potting material into these air spaces.

### Torches for sterilizing tools

Dirty cutting and potting tools can spread diseases. Preventing disease by sterilizing any tools that come in direct contact with orchid root and leaf tissue is always a good idea. You can use chemical solutions to do this (for instance, a 1:10 ratio of household bleach to water), but chemicals are very corrosive and some are toxic. A very simple way to sterilize metal tools is to flame them with a propane or butane torch (see Figure 3-3). Both are available in small handheld sizes.

## Potting supplies

The orchid tag that comes with the orchid or the one you make yourself contains very important information that you want to protect. Knowing the correct name of the orchid is crucial information when you're looking up cultural information. Also, many times the tag includes the orchid's parents' names, which can also provide helpful cultural clues. If you want to enter your orchid in a show, it may be disqualified without proper labeling.

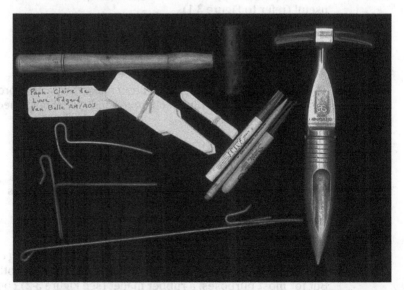

**Figure 3-2:** Potting tools — clockwise from top-left: rubber mallet, dibble, potting clamps, labels, marking pens.

**Figure 3-3:** This compact, lightweight, self-striking butane torch is a breeze to use.

 So the important message is: Keep a legible label in the pots of all your orchids. Maintaining a separate list of your orchids is also a good idea. To make it easier, assign numbers to each of your plants and place this number on the label. This serves as a safety net in case the label is damaged or lost.

### Labels

Many types of labels are available, in all different sizes and colors. Which size or color you choose is a personal choice — the material they're made of is a more important consideration. Table 3-1 lists some pros and cons of each kind of label.

**Table 3-1      Pros and Cons of Various Types of Labels**

| Type | Pros | Cons | Comments |
| --- | --- | --- | --- |
| Metal (copper) | Lasts many years | More expensive<br><br>Not as readily available | Good for very-long-term use<br><br>Is usually thin enough to mark by indenting with a pencil |
| Metal (zinc) | Lasts many years | More expensive<br><br>Not as readily available | Good for very-long-term use<br><br>Can be marked on with #2 lead pencil or engraved |

*(continued)*

## Table 3-1 *(continued)*

| Type | Pros | Cons | Comments |
|------|------|------|----------|
| Plastic | Inexpensive<br><br>Available in largest range of sizes and colors | Becomes brittle (especially if exposed to sunlight) and then breaks very easily | Recommended for short-term use only (less than a few years)<br><br>Will accept a broad range of markers |
| Vinyl | Does not get nearly as brittle as plastic | More expensive than plastic<br><br>Not as readily available | Probably the best overall choice<br><br>Will accept a broad range of markers |
| Wood | Inexpensive<br><br>Readily available | Rots quickly | Because it lasts such a short time in damp orchid potting material, it isn't recommended |

### Label markers

Using the right marker can mean the difference between being able to read the name of the orchid three years after you bought it and not. Table 3-2 lists some advantages and disadvantages of each type.

## Table 3-2 The Pros and Cons of Various Types of Label Markers

| Type | Pros | Cons | Comments |
|------|------|------|----------|
| Engraver | Lasts forever<br><br>Most effective on metal labels, especially zinc | Slow to use<br><br>Difficult to write small letters<br><br>More expensive<br><br>Hard to read after a few years | Handy for long-term labels that are exposed to the elements and chemical sprays |
| Paint pen | Comes in a variety of colors and thicknesses<br><br>Won't fade as badly as permanent markers | Takes longer to dry than permanent markers<br><br>Must be more careful in using them not to smear the paint before it dries | My favorite<br><br>Available at craft and art-supply stores |

| Type | Pros | Cons | Comments |
|------|------|------|----------|
| Pencil | An old-fashioned, but still very effective marker on plastic and vinyl | Not as easy to read as some other markers<br><br>Can smear | Use #2 lead for best legibility |
| Permanent marker | Easy to find and use<br><br>Available in many colors and thicknesses<br><br>Makes dark, visible letters | Will bleach out in sun<br><br>Can also be affected by pesticides | Reasonably good to use but after two or three years may have to be traced over to remain legible<br><br>Some brands have more resistance to sunlight than others |

### Clips and stakes

Numerous types of stakes and clamps are used to hold the orchid in its pot when it has been transplanted and its roots are inadequate, by themselves, to anchor the plant. Figure 3-2 shows some samples of metal stakes. Bamboo stakes are also available.

# Watering Accessories

Mastering the art of watering is one of the critical keys to success in orchid culture (see Chapter 6). These accessories deliver water, and in some cases fertilizer, gently and effectively.

## Water breakers

Water breakers are attached to the end of a hose to diffuse the water and prevent it from washing out the orchid potting material (see Figure 3-4). They deliver a large volume of water, but in a very gentle way — and they work really well.

You can find water breakers that deliver different volumes and water patterns such as mist, fine shower, jet, or flood. Some watering heads can be dialed to whichever of these forms you want — very handy.

You're usually better off choosing the water breaker that delivers the finest steam of water possible. This will be most useful for the broadest range of watering applications.

**Figure 3-4:** A common type of water breaker.

## Water-flow regulators

Water-flow regulators are attached to the hose before the water breaker to regulate the volume of water. The simplest ones are manual on/off valves. I find the thumb or squeeze valves are easiest to use more precisely and determine the volume of water you want to deliver to your orchids (see Figure 3-5).

**Figure 3-5:** Thumb valves make watering easier.

## Hoses

Buy the best-quality hose you can find. The better ones will not kink and will last much longer.

If hoses tend to get in the way, consider the newer "coil" hoses. They take up much less space and can be attached to a sink spigot. Again, buy the best grade you can find — the cheaper ones tend to kink very easily.

## Watering cans

Many of the sprinkling or watering cans on the market are close to worthless for using on orchids. They deliver too much water too fast and are awkward to use in tight indoor spaces. The best type to use, for most situations, is one that holds ½ to 1 gallon (2 to 4 liters), has a long spout (so you can reach orchids in the back row), and has a removable water breaker (sometimes called a *rose*) on the end of its spout that delivers a very fine stream of water (see Figure 3-6). The watering can may be made of metal or plastic, but the water breaker should be made of metal, preferably a nonrusting one, like copper.

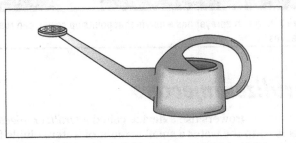

**Figure 3-6:** The most useful watering can is one with a long spout.

## Sprayers and misters

You can use sprayers and misters for misting the orchids to temporarily increase the humidity, to clean the leaves, or for applying pesticides. If you're going to use any chemicals in them, the plastic sprayers are less prone to being affected by these corrosive materials so they're a better choice than metal ones.

One type of hand sprayer that I've found particularly effective for applying insecticides is a teat sprayer because its spray head points up instead of straight forward like standard sprayers. These are actually used to wash off cow udders (hence, the name), so they're sold at farm-supply stores. But for orchid growers, they serve admirably to apply these chemicals to the undersides of leaves, where the bugs usually hang out (see Figure 3-7).

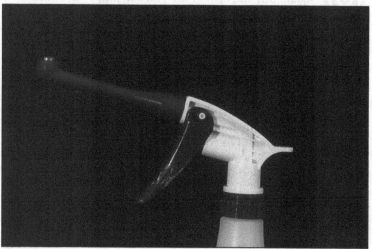

Photograph courtesy of Marc Herzog

**Figure 3-7:** A teat sprayer has a nozzle that points up so you can reach under the leaves.

## Fertilizer injectors

Commercial growers use a device called a *fertilizer injector* that "injects" into the water a small amount of water-soluble fertilizer each time the plant is watered. In this way, the orchids are constantly fed a very diluted amount of fertilizer instead of larger amounts every two weeks or so, as is frequently done. These units tend to be on the expensive side and may be a luxury item, unless you have quite a large number of orchids to fertilize.

A much cheaper way around this is to use a simple siphon mixer. Several brands are on the market, but they all work basically the same. You attach the siphon mixer to the spigot before the hose. A flexible hollow rubber tube is inserted into a concentrated solution of fertilizer. When the spigot is turned, a suction action created by the water flowing through the hose draws this concentrate through the tubing so it flows into the water in the hose and is diluted while it's being applied to the orchid plants.

To get the most benefit from a siphon mixer, here are a few tips:

✓ **Use a completely soluble fertilizer so it won't plug up the unit.**

✓ **Use a water breaker that functions with a low volume of water.** The water flow coming out the end of the hose will be significantly reduced when the siphon mixer is attached.

✓ **Be sure the unit you have also has a backflow preventer.** That way, when you turn off the water breaker, but not the spigot, the back pressure won't cause the concentrated fertilizer solution to flush back into your house water or back into your fertilizer concentrate.

✓ **To be on the safe side, use the siphon mixer only for applying fertilizers, not pesticides.**

✓ **Be careful to dilute the fertilizer to the correct concentration.** These usually inject the fertilizer on a 1:16 fertilizer-to-water ratio, but always read the directions that come with the unit.

## Deionization and reverse osmosis units

Deionization and reverse osmosis units are used to purify your well or tap water to reduce or eliminate concentrations of salts that can be harmful to some particularly sensitive orchids. The units aren't cheap and can be cumbersome and bothersome to use. So, before you consider getting one, make sure you need it.

Here are some things to consider before you buy:

✓ **If your orchids and other houseplants have been growing, then don't worry about using a deionization or reverse osmosis unit.** Most households can get by with the water they have.

✓ **If you've had water problems or just want to be on the safe side, check with your public water provider to see what the average total dissolved solids (TDS) is in your water.** If you have your own well, you'll need to have a test done at a private water lab.

  • If you have 60 parts per million (ppm) or less of TDS and less than 5 ppm of sodium, you're home free. Your water is of good quality for orchids.

  • If your water tests at 60 to 120 ppm and you have up to 10 ppm of sodium, all except the most sensitive orchids should be okay, but you're on the edge with water quality.

> • If you have readings higher than 120 ppm for TDS or
> 10 ppm of sodium, you may have more orchid-growing
> success if you use better-quality water. To do this, you
> could collect rainwater (you can buy special rain barrels
> for this purpose that hook up to your downspout), or
> consider buying a reverse osmosis or deionization unit.
>
> If you're on the higher end of the TDS level, be particularly
> careful not to overfertilize.

# Humidifiers, Heaters, and Ventilation Equipment

Your home environment is designed to make you, not necessarily
your plants, comfortable. Fortunately, many of your living requirements are the same as the living requirements for most of the
orchids in this book. In some cases, though, you'll need to modify
your orchids' growing space to better suit them.

## Humidifiers

The importance of providing sufficient humidity for better health
for both you and your orchids is detailed in Chapter 5. To humidify
an entire room, there are at least three possible approaches, covered in the following sections.

### Evaporative-pad humidifiers

With these units, fans blow across a moisture-laden pad that sits in a
reservoir of water. Evaporative-pad humidifiers are my first choice
for home humidification because

✔ They're reasonably priced and readily available.

✔ They don't spray the room with droplets of water that can
carry mineral deposits and bacteria.

✔ They circulate air at the same time.

✔ They only increase the humidity to about 50 to 60 percent
(most have an adjustable *humidistat,* which measures humidity).
This is a level that is beneficial to plants, but not sufficient to
cause moisture damage to the house.

✔ They require no plumbing and very little maintenance — just
change the moisture pads one or two times a season.

### Cool-mist humidifiers

Cool-mist humidifiers can be effective for small areas, but with constant use, they can cause deposits of minerals on leaves and be a bacteria carrier.

### Greenhouse-type foggers or humidifiers

If you have a greenhouse or a very large growing area that really needs a lot of humidity, a greenhouse-type fogger or humidifier is for you. These units can be pricey. They're plumbed into a constant water supply that is controlled by a float (much like a toilet bowl). The humidity level can be regulated by a separately purchased humidistat.

# Ventilation

Adequate air circulation is very important in orchid culture. Fortunately, many convenient and inexpensive pieces of equipment do this job admirably. Here are some of the best choices:

- ✔ **Ceiling fans:** These are readily available and do a super job of moving large volumes of air in a figure-8 pattern at a low velocity. Most of them have reversible motors, so they can either be set to pull the cooler air from the floor (usually the summer setting) or push hot air down from the ceiling (usually the winter setting).

- ✔ **Oscillating and standard fans:** You can find these in all blade sizes, and most have variable speeds. All will do the job, but you're better off getting one with a larger blade size and running it at low speed. This will move more air but not at as high a velocity, so the plants won't become dehydrated by a strong air current. Also, for oscillating types, splurge on a better-grade model that has metal or heavy-duty gears; otherwise, they'll strip in short order, and you'll then have a stationary fan.

- ✔ **Muffin fans:** These are very small, handy fans (3 to 6 inches/ 8 to 15 cm) that are used to cool electronic equipment like computers. They're great for bringing a gentle, quiet breeze to a small corner of your growing area. You can find them at electronic or computer-supply stores or in catalogs.

For more information on the importance of ventilation and air movement, see Chapter 5.

# Heating

If you're like most people, you'll rely on your home heating system to provide most of the heat for your orchids. You can supplement that with small electric heaters or water-resistant heating mats commonly used to start seeds. If you're growing under lights, you can enclose your growing area in plastic film to help retain heat produced by the lights and ballasts.

# Thermometers and hygrometers

I have to admit, and my wife will quickly concur, that I'm a nut about temperature and humidity monitoring. I've got remote sensors all over my home that tell me maximum and minimum temperature and humidity levels each day. As I explain in Chapter 5, temperature differentials are important to know about if you're interested in getting your orchids to bloom. Thanks to modern digital thermometers and hygrometers that are simple to use and not expensive, you can keep track of temperature and humidity with little effort.

# Chapter 4

# How I Love Thy Orchid: Enjoying the Orchid's Beauty

. . . . . . . . . . . . . . . . . . . . . . . . . . . . . . . . . . . . . . . . . .

## In This Chapter

▶ Caring for your orchids in their new home

▶ Staking your orchids when they bloom

▶ Showing off your orchids in your home

▶ Making beautiful orchid flower arrangements

▶ Getting the most mileage out of your orchid flowers

. . . . . . . . . . . . . . . . . . . . . . . . . . . . . . . . . . . . . . . . . .

The main purpose for growing orchids is to enjoy their unmatched beauty in your home. In this chapter, I walk you through tips that will make your experiences with orchids more successful and pleasurable.

## Caring for Orchids in Their New Home

Bringing an orchid plant into its new home can be traumatic for both the plant and you! You have to get to know each other. Most orchids you buy will have come from a very high-light, high-humidity environment of a commercial greenhouse. You bring them into your home environment, which is usually less bright with lower humidity, so the plant has to make some adjustments. Doing this with the least amount of distress is your goal, and in this section, I help you get there.

In Chapter 5, I give you the details of routine orchid care, but here I want to give you some tips that will make the short-term transition easier for both of you.

## *If the plant is in bloom*

Here are some tips that will make the flowers on your new orchid last longer:

- ✔ **Place the plant somewhere in your house that's bright, but where it won't get direct sunlight, except possibly in the morning.** Too much harsh sunlight can bleach out the flowers.

- ✔ **Keep the plant on the cool side — not above about 75°F (about 24°C).** Flowers stay fresher longer this way.

- ✔ **Be sure to keep the plant well watered.** Even though the orchid plant stops growing much when it's in bloom, the leaves and flowers still need water.

- ✔ **Don't let any bees or flies in the room where your orchids are blooming.** If the bees or flies pollinate them, the flowers will collapse afterward.

- ✔ **Don't put the plant close to ripe fruit.** Fruit gives off ethylene gas, which can cause flowers to collapse prematurely.

- ✔ **Keep your orchid plants away from strong fumes like paint thinners or other pollutants.** These can cause the blossoms to fade.

- ✔ **Don't spray the flowers with water or place the blooming plant in a room that is highly humid with no air movement.** This can cause spotting on the flowers from fungal diseases.

## *If the plant is not in bloom*

Before you add your new, not-yet-blooming orchid to your collection, follow these tips:

- ✔ **Look under the leaves and at the younger growth to make sure there are no bugs.**

- ✔ **To be on the safe side, isolate this new plant from your collection for at least three weeks.** This will allow time for hidden insect eggs to hatch out.

- ✔ **As a further precaution, spray the plant thoroughly with an insecticidal soap.** Use a paper towel to wipe off the excess spray. This will not only kill any soft-bodied insects but will also clean the leaves.

- ✔ **Consider repotting the orchid into your own potting mix.** That way you'll be assured that the potting mix is fresh and you'll know its watering requirements.

# Staking and Grooming Your Blooming Orchids

Orchids deserve to look their best when they're putting on their show. Proper staking and grooming can make a big difference in how orchid flowers appear.

## Figuring out how to stake

Flowers and spikes of orchids can be heavy and, if they aren't staked properly, they'll open at an awkward and disconcerting angle. This can be a distraction, because the most interesting and alluring perspective to view orchids is usually the head-on view.

Staking techniques vary somewhat with the type of orchid. The two major types are the spray orchids, like phalaenopsis and oncidiums, or those with single flowers or just a few on one spike, like cattleyas and most paphiopedilums.

### For spray-type orchids

Be sure to start this process *before* these orchids are actually in flower. This will ensure that the flowers are oriented correctly when they open. Here are the steps I recommend:

1. **As soon as the flower spike is about 12 inches (30 cm) long, insert a vertical bamboo stake (you can get a green one, so it blends in better) close to where the spike originates at the base of the plant (see Figure 4-1).**

2. **As you insert the stake, twist it to work it around roots to minimize damage to them.**

3. **Attach the first tie on the lower part of the spike close to the first *node* (the bump in the flower stem).**

   Use twist-ties or Velcro, not sharp string or wire, which could damage the stem.

4. **Attach another tie a few inches higher on the flower spike.**

5. **Put additional ties every few inches as the flower spike grows.**

6. **Place the last tie a few inches below where the first flower buds are forming.**

   This allows the spike to form a natural arch with the first flower open at the highest point and the others gracefully following suit right below that one.

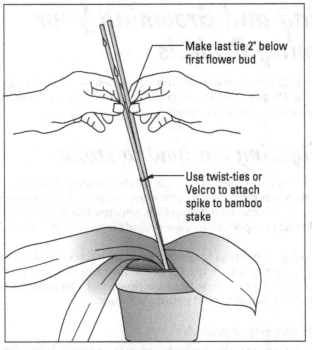

Make last tie 2" below first flower bud

Use twist-ties or Velcro to attach spike to bamboo stake

**Figure 4-1:** Staking flower spikes of spray-type orchids like phalaenopsis or oncidiums.

Flower spikes always grow in the direction of the strongest light. After the flower spike reaches about 12 inches (30 cm) tall and the buds are starting to form, *never* change the plant's orientation to the light source. If you do, the spike will try to reorient itself and you'll end up with a twisted, distorted spike with flowers opening in all directions.

When the flowers are fully open, they'll stay that way, so you can then move the plant anywhere you want.

### For single- or few-flowered orchids

Staking these orchids is simpler. When the bud or buds start to swell on the flower spike, insert a vertical bamboo stake close to where the spike originates at the base of the plant.

Be sure to do this before the flower has opened so that the bud will orient itself to gravity. If the flower spike is at an angle, the flower will adjust itself to open perpendicular to the angle the flower stem is pointing. If you tie the spike up after it has opened, it will keep its original orientation and will look awkward.

In the last few years, orchid growers have discovered one of the best ways to attach upright flowering stems to bamboo or wood stakes: spring-operated baby hair clips! They're available in all colors, are inexpensive, and frequently are formed in whimsical shapes of butterflies or dragonflies, which fit well with the orchid look. Plus, they work well!

## Helping your orchids look their best

After growing the plants for months on the windowsill, under lights, or in a greenhouse, they can look a little rough around the edges. The leaves are probably dusty and/or blemished with chemical deposits, older leaves may be wilted or dead, and some of the tips of the leaves may be brown.

When the plants are in flower and you want to show them off to their best in your home or get them ready to exhibit in an orchid show, here are a few suggestions to keep in mind:

✔ **Clean their leaves.** A simple way to polish the leaves is with milk. Dampen a paper towel with milk and rub off the blemishes. This will give a very attractive sheen that is harmless to the plant.

✔ **Carefully remove any dead or severely damaged leaves.**

✔ **If you're planning to bring your orchid to a show, be sure that you tape to the pot the name of your orchid plus your own name so that you don't lose the plant.** Also, make a list of what plants you've entered so you have a record.

✔ **Trim off the brown tips of leaves with very sharp scissors.** The sharper they are, the cleaner the cut and the less leaf-tissue damage will result. When trimming, follow the natural shape of the leaf, as shown in Figure 4-2.

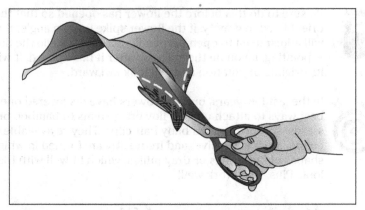

**Figure 4-2:** Trim off brown tips of leaves following the natural curvature of the leaf.

## Displaying orchid plants in your home

When you're showing off your prized blooming plants in your home, here a few tips to keep in mind:

- ✔ Be sure to protect your furniture by placing the orchid plant pots on waterproof pads, like cork platters.

- ✔ If you place your plants on saucers, be sure they're waterproof. Terra cotta platters are porous and moisture will seep through and can cause serious damage to unprotected wood furniture.

- ✔ Place felt or rubber protectors under cachepots, platters, or saucers so your furniture won't be scratched.

- ✔ Place the blooming plants where they get bright light but not hot, late-afternoon light, so the flowers will last longer.

- ✔ If the growing pot is encrusted or ugly, insert it into a larger ornamental pot or basket. Choose simple green, white, or neutral colors that don't compete with the orchid flowers.

- ✔ Place a layer of sheet moss or Spanish moss on the surface of the pot. This is a nice touch for covering up the sometimes unattractive potting material.

✔ **Display the orchid on a pedestal or higher elevation so you can view it at eye level (see Figure 4-3).** Few orchids are as attractive when they're viewed from above.

✔ **Think about how you will light your orchids to display them best.** Many people are only able to view their orchids during the work week in the evening, so artificial lighting plays an important part in viewing them. Track lights work great. Use halogen or other bulbs that produce white light or as close to sunlight as possible so the orchid flowers will be rendered accurately. Regular incandescent light produces a yellow/red light that will make reds glow but that really dulls blues and greens.

✔ **Group orchids with other tropical foliage plants.** These provide an attractive backdrop for the orchid flowers.

**Figure 4-3:** Placing plants on pedestals and inserting their growing pot inside a more ornamental one draws attention to the best attributes of the orchids — their flowers.

## Arranging orchid flowers

Nothing is more elegant than orchids in a flower arrangement. They've always represented the pinnacle of good taste and sophistication. The key to using them for such purposes is to keep it simple and not to let the elegance of the orchids get overwhelmed by too many other elements.

# A super-simple homemade orchid flower preservative

Here's an easy recipe for making your cut orchids last longer. Combine one 12-ounce can of a lemon-flavored soda drink (like Sprite or 7-Up), an equal quantity of water, and 1 teaspoon of household bleach. The sugar in the soft drink serves as food for the flower, the citric acid lowers the pH (increases the acidity), and the bleach kills the bacteria in the water that can plug up the water-conducting network in the flower stem.

## Understanding the three basic flower-design elements

When it comes to flower arranging, flowers and greens comes in three basic shapes — line, mass, and filler. All of these play a key part in the construction of an attractive flower arrangement:

- ✔ **Line flowers** are tall and are used to give your arrangement height and width. Various branched orchids with buds (for example, oncidiums and cymbidiums) are used to create this effect.

- ✔ **Mass flowers** give your bouquet weight or mass and are generally round or full-faced. They're usually the focal point of color and interest in a bouquet. Examples are cattleyas and their relatives, as well as paphiopedilums and angraecums.

- ✔ **Filler flowers** have stems with many little flowers and usually have fine textured foliage. Examples are miniature oncidiums.

Here are some tips on how to make simple, yet elegant, arrangements:

- ✔ **Line flowers, by themselves, can make a striking arrangement in a tall, cylindrical vase.** Select a vase or container that is in proportion to the flowers. The vase should be about one-half to one-third the size of the total arrangement. For instance, 3-foot-tall spikes of cymbidiums or oncidiums need a vase 12 to 18 inches tall.

- ✔ **You can arrange mass flowers by themselves in a low, wide vase or container (see Figure 4-4).**

- ✔ **A small arrangement of filler flowers by themselves can add a light, elegant touch to any room.** Many of these filler flowers are well suited for drying.

✓ **Some flowers can be used as more than one element.** For example, phalaenopsis sprays, especially the multifloral types, can be used as line elements, while large single flowers can be used as mass flowers.

**Figure 4-4:** This miniature arrangement contains only three small cattleya flowers for the mass and three pointed leaves for the line element.

## Supporting the orchid flower stems

Having some method of supporting the stems of orchids in an arrangement, so you can arrange them to face the direction you prefer, is usually a good idea. Here are several methods and materials you can use:

✓ **For a clear vase, add marbles or rocks.**

✓ **Crossing the top opening of the vase in a tic-tac-toe pattern of florist's tape works well.**

✓ *Frogs* **(pincushions on which the orchid stems are impaled) work well in shallower containers.**

✓ **Florist foam is most popular with professional arrangers because it's easy to use, effective, and retains water well so that the flowers last.** It's usually used in low containers.

Don't cut the orchid flowers until they're fully open. Otherwise, they may never have their proper shape or complete color.

### Making your orchid arrangement last longer

To make your cut flowers last longer, follow these suggestions:

- ✔ **For cymbidiums, wait about ten days to two weeks after they've flowered before cutting; for cattleyas, wait several days.** Cut the orchids only when they've fully opened.

- ✔ **Before you put the orchids into a vase, their stems should be recut at an angle *under* water.** To keep them fresh, recut them every several days.

- ✔ **Condition the orchids first, before arranging them.** Place their stems in warm (180°F/82°C), fresh water and let them sit somewhere cool (around 50°F/10°C) overnight.

- ✔ **Make sure all leaves that will be submerged under water in the vase are removed.**

- ✔ **To use orchids' short stems (like cattleyas) in taller arrangements, insert the flower stem into *orchid tubes* (water-holding test tubes, available at your local florist) and then tape the tubes to a wood stake for more height.**

- ✔ **Add a commercial or homemade solution of floral preservative (see the nearby sidebar) to the warm water containing the flowers.** Change this water and solution every three to four days.

- ✔ **Place the arrangement out of the direct rays of sunlight and in a cool room.**

- ✔ **Double the life of your orchid flowers by placing the arrangement in the refrigerator at night or when you're away from home.**

# Part II
# The Basics of Orchid Parenthood

"To our new neighbors. May you enjoy your new home, and keep your dog out of our flower beds."

## In this part . . .

Growing orchids is easy, but as with anything, you need to know the right things to do or not to do.

In this part, I tell you what environments orchids prefer and give you all you need to know to make your home the perfect growing space for these tropical beauties. You'll find information on light, humidity, temperature, and ventilation requirements. I cover proper watering in detail, a big problem for many beginners. I also demystify the process of purchasing and using fertilizers on orchids.

Dividing and repotting orchids is a daunting task for many new growers. In this part, I give you detailed drawings showing you step-by-step methods and techniques to use for various types of orchids, so you can do this job with no fear.

One great aspect of orchids is that they get bigger and better every year. When this happens, you have the opportunity to multiply your orchids and share them with friends or use them for trading for other desired varieties. I'll show you, in detail, various ways to do this.

Healthy orchids are happy orchids. Fortunately, orchids are not a buggy lot, but they sometimes do succumb to various diseases and insects. I show you the safe and effective way to keep these unwanted organisms in check.

After reading Part II, you'll be ready to grow orchids as the pros do.

# Chapter 5

# Providing the Right Growing Environment

• • • • • • • • • • • • • • • • • • • • • • • • • • • • • • • • • • • • • • • •

*In This Chapter*

▶ Knowing how much light your orchid needs

▶ Providing enough humidity

▶ Giving your orchids a breath of fresh air

▶ Getting the temperature right

• • • • • • • • • • • • • • • • • • • • • • • • • • • • • • • • • • • • • • • •

*O*rchids are not difficult to grow. But, like all plants, they have certain needs that have to be met so they can perform their best. In this chapter, I detail orchids' most fundamental requirements and the simplest, most effective ways to provide them, based on my 40 years of experience growing orchids on my windowsills, under lights, and in a greenhouse.

If you put a little effort into modifying your growing environment to help your orchids feel at home, it'll pay off in healthy plants that provide plenty of flowers.

## Let There Be Light!

Light is essential for all green plants, including orchids. Light, water, and carbon dioxide are the raw materials plants use to produce their food. Providing enough light is the most challenging requirement for indoor gardeners in areas of the country like the Northeast and the Midwest, who experience short days and low light during the winter. Fortunately, plenty of species and hybrids of orchids don't require super-high light intensities and so are more suited to these climates.

If you're blessed with naturally high light — like the kind found in Hawaii, California, and Florida — you can grow both the high- and the low-light-intensity orchids. You just have to use greenhouse shading or light-reducing draperies to satisfy those orchids requiring modest amounts of light.

## The ins and outs of light

Orchids are traditionally categorized by their light requirements — high, medium, and low. Turn to Chapter 2 for a simple way to determine the intensity of your light source, called the shadow test. Most orchids are in the medium light category. You can easily grow orchids in the low to medium light categories under artificial lights or on bright windowsills. From a practical point of view, the orchids with high light requirements are most successfully grown in bright greenhouses.

### Greenhouses: Your high light source

Greenhouses, like the one shown in Figure 5-1, are the most efficient collectors of natural light.

The amount of light penetrating the greenhouse is determined by the glazing material used, its geographic location, how it's sited on the land, and whether it's shaded by surrounding trees or a commercial shading compound or fabric.

The greenhouse option is the most expensive, but you don't have to own one to grow most of the orchids in this book.

**Figure 5-1:** High-quality greenhouse setups provide shading and efficient use of space to accommodate as many orchids as possible.

## *Windowsills: Not all windowsills are created equal*

Windowsills are the most readily available and cost-effective source of light. The amount of light windowsill growing can provide is primarily determined by

✔ **The size of the windows.**

✔ **Whether there is an overhanging roof:** This can make a difference in how much light will actually reach the plants (see Figure 5-2).

✔ **How far back the windows are recessed:** Bay or bow windows expose the plants to more light than other types of windows (see Figure 5-3).

✔ **The direction the windows face:** Whether the windows face north, south, east, or west makes a big difference in the amount and quality of light the orchids will receive:

- **South-facing window:** This is the brightest window, so it offers the most possibilities. It's an ideal location for orchids that demand the strongest light. You can place most of the other less-light-demanding orchids a few feet back from the window, or you can diffuse the light from the window with a sheer curtain. *Note:* This exposure can get hot, especially during the summer.

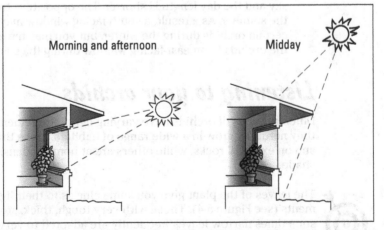

Morning and afternoon          Midday

**Figure 5-2:** The extent of the roof overhang will make a difference in the amount of light the orchids will receive.

- **East-facing window:** This window offers morning sunlight, which is bright but not too hot. During the spring, summer, and fall, this is usually an ideal exposure for most orchids in this book, except those that require extremely high light (like vandas). During the short, dark days of winter, many of these same orchids usually prefer a south-facing window.

- **West-facing window:** This window receives as much light as the east window but, because it gets afternoon light, it's much hotter — so this isn't as desirable a location as the east-facing window. If you need to use a west-facing window, make sure your orchids don't dry out too much because of this increased heat.

- **North-facing window:** A north-facing window simply doesn't provide enough light to sustain the healthy growth of orchids. Use it for low-light plants like ferns.

✔ **How far the plants are placed from the windows.**

✔ **The age and condition of the glass:** Tinted and reflective glass can dramatically reduce light intensity, so it's usually not recommended. No matter what kind of glass you have, keep your windows clean, especially during the winter when the light intensity is low, so your orchids will receive as much light as possible.

✔ **The time of the year:** During the winter, the sun is lower in the sky and the day length is shorter. The opposite is true during the summer. As a result, a south-facing window may be fine for certain orchids during the winter, but you may have to move the orchids to an east-facing window during the summer.

## Listening to your orchids

Different types of orchids have varying light requirements because they naturally grow in a wide range of habitats. Some thrive in full sun on exposed rocks, while others are at home in dense jungle shade.

The leaves of the plant give you some clue as to their light requirements (see Figure 5-4). Those with very tough, thick, stout, and sometimes narrow leaves frequently are adapted to very high light intensity. When the leaves are softer, more succulent, and wider, this is usually a clue that they're from a lower-light environment.

**Figure 5-3:** Bay windows increase the size of the growing area and the amount of light the plant receives, because light can penetrate from multiple angles.

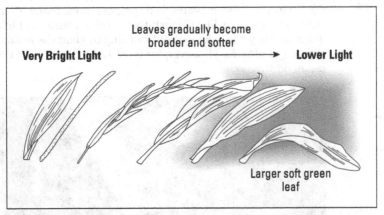

Leaves gradually become broader and softer

**Very Bright Light** ⟶ **Lower Light**

Larger soft green leaf

**Figure 5-4:** The type of leaf indicates an orchid's light requirements.

Your orchids will tell you by their growth habits and leaf color if they're getting adequate, too little, or too much light. When orchids are getting enough light, you'll notice the following:

✔ The mature leaves are usually a medium to light green.

✔ The new leaves are the same size or larger and the same shape as the mature ones.

✔ The foliage is stiff and compact, not floppy.

✔ The plants are flowering at approximately the same time they did the year before.

One of the most frequent results of inadequate light is soft, dark green foliage with no flowering. Another symptom of inadequate light is *stretching,* where the distance between the new leaves on the stem of orchids like paphiopedilum, phalaenopsis, or vandas is greater than with the older, mature leaves. On other types of orchids, the new leaves tend to be longer and thinner.

When orchids get too much light, their leaves turn a yellow-green color or take on a reddish cast and may appear stunted. In extreme cases, the leaves show circular or oval sunburn spots (see Figure 5-5). The sunburn is actually caused by the leaf overheating. Although, in itself, this leaf damage may not cause extreme harm to the plant if the damage is isolated to a small area, it does make the plant unsightly.

If the sunburn occurs at the growing point, it can kill that leaf or the entire plant. Higher light intensities than are usually recommended are possible with some orchids if you increase the ventilation to lower these elevated leaf temperatures. Some orchid cut-flower growers like to push their orchids with the highest light intensity they can take without burning to yield the maximum amount of blooms. However, for most hobby growers, I don't recommend this.

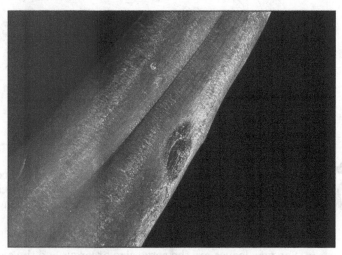

**Figure 5-5:** A paphiopedilum leaf with a round or oval brown spot caused by too much light or sunburn.

# No natural light? No problem!

Artificial light sources make it possible for everyone without green-houses or bright windowsills to enjoy growing orchids in their homes. Although the limitations of what can be grown under these light sources are only restricted by equipment and electricity costs, it's a very practical method of growing for low- to medium-light orchids.

Wading through the many lighting options available today can be a daunting task, especially for beginners. In this section, I help you out.

## Fluorescent lights

Fluorescent systems are still the most accessible and economical lighting systems to buy. Three-tiered light carts, like the one shown in Figure 5-6, are highly versatile and practical. Most of them are about 2 feet wide by 4 feet long, so their three shelves provide 24 square feet of growing area. If you grow compact orchids, this will be enough space to have at least one or more orchids in bloom year-round. If you collect miniatures, it will provide a growing space adequate for an entire collection. The convenience of such a cart can't be beat. You can place it in a heated garage, in a basement, or in a spare bedroom.

When the orchids start to produce their tall orchid spikes, there usually isn't enough head room under most fixed-height light units to accommodate this growing spike. At that point, you can move the orchids to a windowsill or use a light fixture that can be raised as the flower spikes develop, like the one shown in Figure 5-7.

Which bulbs or lamps you should burn in your fixtures is a highly debated topic. Years ago, the only real choice was cool white and warm white tubes. Some people still feel that a 50/50 mix of these tubes is the best option, because they're bright and very inexpensive.

Over 40 years ago, Sylvania started manufacturing Gro-Lux tubes — designed to provide light that more closely reflected the spectrum of light that plants used in *photosynthesis,* the process that plants use to produce their own food. This started a new race to produce the "best" plant bulb. The evolution of lamps has gone from the Gro-Lux to wide-spectrum bulbs and now to full-spectrum bulbs. The light cast by the full-spectrum lamp is supposed to most closely resemble natural sunlight. Viewed under these lamps, colors of the flowers are rendered more accurately.

**Figure 5-6:** Four-tube, rather than two-tube, units are highly recommended for low- to medium-light orchids.

**Figure 5-7:** An adjustable light fixture like this one is very handy for accommodating developing flower spikes.

I've grown orchids well under all these types of lamps. If you want to have the flowers appear most naturally colored under the lights and don't mind paying a premium for the lamps, the full-spectrum types are the best choice. The most economical pick — and still satisfactory — is the 50/50 ratio of warm-white to cool-white lamps. A compromise would be a blend of half warm-white and cool-white tubes and half wide- or full-spectrum lamps.

### High-intensity-discharge lights

Newer to the artificial-light choices are high-intensity-discharge lights. These are very efficient in their production of light and are especially useful where you want to grow orchids requiring higher light intensities than fluorescent lamps can provide and/or where you want a greater working distance between the lights and plants (see Figure 5-8).

High-intensity-discharge lights do have the disadvantage of producing quite a bit of heat, so make sure not to get the plants too close to the bulbs.

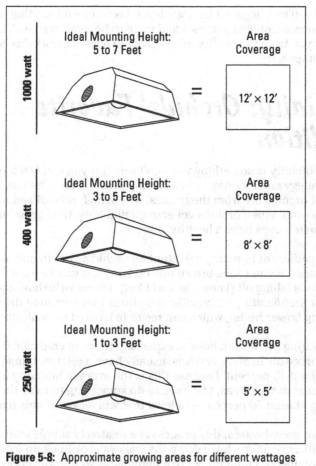

**Figure 5-8:** Approximate growing areas for different wattages of high-intensity-discharge lamps.

The two most frequently used lamps for these systems are metal halide (MH) and high-pressure sodium (HPS). HPS is more energy-efficient than MH, but the light it emits is orange-yellow and distorts the color of the flowers and foliage. MH produces blue light that is more pleasing to the eye. Some manufacturers now produce lamps that combine the advantages of both.

Another newer option is the high-intensity compact fluorescent light. The fixtures for these look much like high-intensity-discharge (HID) units. They don't produce quite as much light as HID, but they have the advantage of producing little heat — so there is much less likelihood of orchids being burned.

If you're a beginner light gardener, I recommend starting with fluorescent-light setups. I find them to be most practical. Later, if you have the need, you can give the high-intensity-discharge lamps a try.

# Humidity: Orchids' Favorite Condition

Humidity is something you can't see, but you can feel it on a muggy summer day or in a steamy greenhouse. The vast majority of orchids are from the tropics, where high rainfall and humidity prevail. When orchids get enough humidity, they grow lushly and their leaves have a healthy shine.

Insufficient humidity can stunt an orchid's growth and, in severe cases, it can cause brown tips on leaves. It can also contribute to buds falling off (known as *bud blast*), leaves wrinkling, and drying of the *sheaths* (the tubelike structures that surround the developing flower buds), which can result in twisted or malformed flowers.

During the winter, homes, especially those in cold climates with forced-air heating systems, usually have a relative humidity of about 15 percent. Because this is the average humidity found in most desert areas, you have to do something to raise the humidity to at least 50 percent — a level that will make orchids happy.

For greenhouses, this process is a relatively simple matter. You can either regularly hose down the walkways or hook up foggers and commercial humidifiers to a humidistat so that the entire operation is automatic.

If you're growing your orchids in your home, you'll need a different approach. High humidity levels that would be no problem in a greenhouse will peel the paint, plaster, and wallpaper off the walls of your house. Assuming that's not the look you're going for, you can take several steps to get to the desirable humidity range without causing damage to your house.

If you can, put your orchids in a naturally damp area, like the basement.

Wherever you put your orchids, use a room humidifier. I find the best type of humidifier is an *evaporative-pad humidifier* (in which fans blow across a moisture-laden pad that sits in a reservoir of water). An evaporative-pad humidifier is usually better than a mist humidifier, because, unlike a mist humidifier, it doesn't leave your orchids with a white film (from the minerals in the water being deposited on the leaves).

To further increase the humidity level, you can try growing the plants on top of a waterproof tray filled with pebbles. Add water to the tray so that the level is just below the surface of the pebbles, then put the plants on top of this bed of damp gravel. The problem that I find with this system is that the pots, especially the heavy clay ones, frequently sink into the pebbles, resulting in the media in the pots getting soggy and, after repeated waterings, the pebbles becoming clogged with algae and being a repository for insects and various disease organisms.

The approach that I think works much better is to add sections of egg-crate louvers (sold in home-supply stores for diffusing fluorescent lights) to the trays (see Figure 5-9). You can cut this material with a hacksaw to whatever size you need. It's rigid so it will support the plants above the water, and the water is more exposed to air, so more humidity results. The grating is simple to clean — just remove and spray it with warm water. To prevent algae or disease buildup, you can add a disinfectant like Physan to the water in the trays.

Misting is another way to increase humidity. This works okay, but in order for it to be effective, you need to do it several times a day, because the water usually evaporates very quickly. A problem with misting is that, if your water source is mineral-laden, your orchid's leaves may become encrusted in white — not only is this unsightly, but it keeps light from penetrating to the leaves. A benefit to misting is that it can clean the dust from the leaves.

**Figure 5-9:** An egg-crate louver set inside a waterproof tray. This setup is a simple way to increase humidity, and it's easy to keep clean.

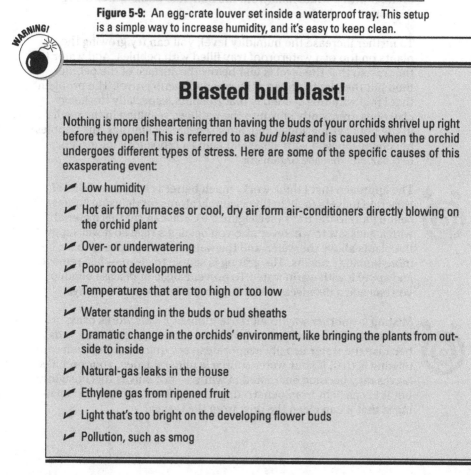

**WARNING!**

# Blasted bud blast!

Nothing is more disheartening than having the buds of your orchids shrivel up right before they open! This is referred to as *bud blast* and is caused when the orchid undergoes different types of stress. Here are some of the specific causes of this exasperating event:

- ✔ Low humidity
- ✔ Hot air from furnaces or cool, dry air form air-conditioners directly blowing on the orchid plant
- ✔ Over- or underwatering
- ✔ Poor root development
- ✔ Temperatures that are too high or too low
- ✔ Water standing in the buds or bud sheaths
- ✔ Dramatic change in the orchids' environment, like bringing the plants from outside to inside
- ✔ Natural-gas leaks in the house
- ✔ Ethylene gas from ripened fruit
- ✔ Light that's too bright on the developing flower buds
- ✔ Pollution, such as smog

# Fresh Air, Please!

In most tropical lands where orchids reside, they luxuriate in incessant, but gentle, trade winds. Air movement in a growing environment ensures a more uniform air temperature and dramatically reduces disease problems by preventing the leaves from staying wet too long. It also evenly distributes the gas (carbon dioxide) that is produced by the plants in the dark and used by the plants to produce their food during the daylight hours.

 You don't want to create gale-force winds in your growing area, but you do want to produce enough airflow to cause the leaves of the orchids to very lightly sway in the breeze. I've found that two of the most effective methods for providing such an airflow in both a hobby greenhouse and an indoor growing area are ceiling fans and oscillating fans.

## Ceiling fans

Ceiling fans move a huge volume of air at a low velocity in a circular pattern, so they effectively prevent severe temperature differences, are inexpensive to operate (they use about the same electricity as a 100-watt bulb), are quiet, have variable speeds, and are easy to install. They stand up well to moist conditions, especially if you buy the outdoor types. Another nice feature is that you can adjust the air-circulation pattern on most of them so that they can either push warm air down (the recommended winter setting) or pull cool air up (usually the best summer setting), as shown in Figure 5-10.

## Oscillating fans

Oscillating fans are also a good choice, because they effectively cover large areas with a constantly changing airflow pattern without excessively drying off the plants.

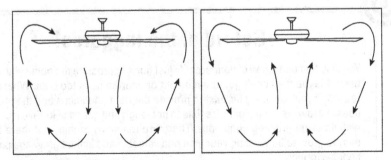

**Figure 5-10:** Ceiling fans can be set either to push warm air down (best for winter) or pull cool air up (best for summer).

If you decide to go with oscillating fans, splurge for the better-grade ones. Fans that are very inexpensive have plastic gears that strip easily, so the oscillating feature won't last long.

## Muffin fans

You may have small hot or cold spots in your greenhouse, windowsill, or light cart where just a touch of airflow is needed. This is where small muffin fans, frequently sold for cooling computers (available at electronics or computer-supply stores), are perfect for the job. They're efficient, quiet, and very inexpensive to operate.

# Some Like It Hot, Some Like It Cold: Orchid Temperature Requirements

Orchids are frequently placed by professional orchid growers into three different categories based on their *night* temperature preferences:

- ✔ **Cool:** 45°F to 55°F (7.2°C to 12.8°C)
- ✔ **Intermediate:** 55°F to 60°F (12.8°C to 15.6°C)
- ✔ **Warm:** 65°F (18.3°C) or higher

The assumption is that the *daytime* temperature will be at least 15°F (9.5°C) warmer than these night temperatures.

These numbers are guidelines, not absolutes. Most orchids are quite adaptable and tolerant of varying temperatures, short of freezing. But for optimum growth, these temperature ranges are good targets.

## Get rid of the laggards!

You may find that a few of your orchids just don't appreciate the home you've given them. Maybe they don't get enough light or your home is too cool. Whatever the reason, if you've done your best to provide the right conditions and the orchid still doesn't grow well and bloom, it's time to get tough and get rid of it! Give it to a friend with different growing conditions. There are too many orchids out there that are easy to grow to be wasting your time and valuable and limited growing space on a poor performer.

## Too-low temperatures

If orchids are exposed to cooler than the recommended ranges, their growth will be slowed down and, in extreme cases, buds may fall off before they open (known as *bud blast*). Also, cooler temperatures can reduce the plant's disease resistance.

## Too-high temperatures

If it gets too hot, orchids will show their displeasure by slowing or stopping their growth, having their flower buds wilt before they open, having their leaves and stems shrivel, and in extreme cases, by dying. A short bout of higher-than-desired temperatures won't be that harmful as long as the humidity stays high.

One critically important factor with orchids is that they need at least 15°F higher daytime temperatures than they get in the evening. If they don't get this temperature difference, the orchids won't grow vigorously and, probably most importantly, they won't set flower buds. Not meeting this temperature requirement is one of the most common reasons that homegrown orchids don't bloom.

# Giving Your Orchids a Summer Vacation

Some orchid growers continue growing their plants indoors under lights, on windowsills, or in their greenhouses throughout the summer. The challenge during this time is to reduce the light intensity and control the high heat, both of which can be damaging.

For these reasons, summering the orchids outdoors is an attractive option. For the light gardener, this means a welcome relief from high electric bills; and for the greenhouse and windowsill grower, it provides an opportunity to clean up the growing area. Also, most orchids aren't in bloom during the summer, so they aren't at their best visually and they respond very favorably to a summer vacation outdoors.

Besides providing an opportunity to clean up your indoor growing area, having a space outdoors allows you to apply pest controls, if necessary, without smelling up your house. The natural temperature differential between day and night, especially in the early fall, is very effective in setting flower buds for the upcoming late-fall and winter blooming.

## A shade house

I summer my orchids in a shade house made of preconstructed *lath* (slates of crisscrossed wood), nailed or screwed to pressure-treated upright wood supports. Figures 5-11 and 5-12 show what my shade house looks like.

Shading (usually about 50 to 60 percent or more depending on the location of the shade house and the types of orchids grown) is necessary and is provided by lath or shading fabrics. I also installed in this shade house a watering system made up of multiple small sprayers or misters controlled by a timer that has a manual override. I grow the plants on stepped wire frame benches that ensure even lighting and easy watering.

**Figure 5-11:** My shade house is an 8-foot (2.4-m) square simply constructed using wood lath and 4-x-4-inch (10-x-10-cm) pressure-treated wood posts.

I cover the roof of the shade house with 6 mil (0.006-mm-thick) heavy-duty clear plastic, which is stretched over a peaked wooden frame. I used to leave the roof of the lath house open to receive natural rainfall, but I found that it sometimes rained when I didn't want it to (at night, when it was too cool, or when it was already wet). I find the covered roof gives me the control to water when my plants need it.

**Figure 5-12:** Inside the shade house, plants are arranged on stepped-wire benches to allow easy watering and good air and water drainage.

## A portable greenhouse

I've also summered orchids in a portable greenhouse on the deck (see Figure 5-13). If you use such a structure, be sure to put it in a place that receives shade during the heat of the day, or use a commercial shading fabric to cut down the light intensity. Also, be mindful of the daytime temperatures inside such a structure. These units require good systems of ventilation; otherwise, temperatures inside them can skyrocket in sunny periods.

# Keeping things in balance: The yin and the yang of orchid growing

When it comes to your orchids' growing conditions, it's a matter of keeping everything in balance. Here are some tips to keep in mind:

- ✔ If the air temperature is cool, the orchids need less water and light.
- ✔ If the humidity is high, the orchids need more air circulation.
- ✔ If the light is very bright and/or the temperature is high, the humidity needs to be high.
- ✔ When orchids are not actively growing, reduce or stop fertilizing.
- ✔ If the temperatures are high, the light and humidity need to also be high and the orchids will require more-frequent watering.

**Figure 5-13:** An outdoor portable greenhouse can be an ideal place to put your orchids in the summer.

## Some orchids enjoy hanging out

Orchids that have higher light requirements, like vandas and asco-cendas, grow wonderfully dangling from pot hangers clipped to the pot (see Figure 5-14) and then hung from a pole or other support. Just make sure the light intensity of this growing area matches the needs of the orchids.

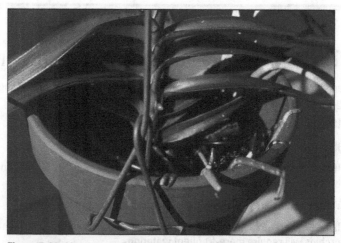

**Figure 5-14:** You can easily summer your orchids outdoors by using pot clamps to hang them from a freestanding support or a suspended rod against the garage.

# Chapter 6

# Watering and Fertilizing Orchids

## In This Chapter

▶ Mastering the art of watering

▶ Knowing when and how to water

▶ Recognizing symptoms of over- and underwatering

▶ Selecting and using orchid fertilizers

*P*robably more orchids are killed by improper watering, usually by overwatering, than by any other cultural practice. Discovering how to properly water orchids is one of the more challenging aspects of growing orchids. In this chapter, I explain some simple but very effective methods that will turn you into a watering pro.

In addition to mastering the art of watering, the fertilizing game can be very confusing — so many different types and formulations! In this chapter, I show you how to wade through the maze of fertilizer terms to get to the important information — you'll be able to choose the fertilizer that will give you healthy orchids with the best blooming.

# Water Water Everywhere: Understanding the Art of Watering Orchids

When I give talks about orchids, one of the first questions asked by those in the audience is, "How often should I water my orchids?" I really wish this question had an easy answer, but it doesn't. So many variables are involved in watering. In the following sections, I cover some of the factors that affect how often you should water.

## The type of pot

You can grow orchids in clay or plastic pots. The potting material dries off much more slowly in plastic pots than it does in clay pots. With plastic, the potting material dries out from the top down, so even though the potting material may be dry on top, it may be damp 1 inch below the surface. With clay pots, the potting material dries out more uniformly (clay pots are porous, so they "breathe" and allow water to evaporate through the walls of the pot).

The bottom line: If you're using a plastic pot, you'll want to water less often than if you're using a clay pot.

Either type of pot will grow orchids, they merely have different watering requirements. For orchids that do best when they're always slightly damp (like miltonias, slippers, and moth orchids), I prefer to use plastic pots. For those that need to dry out more between waterings (like cattleyas and most of the dendrobiums), I recommend clay pots.

In Part III, I provide an overview of numerous orchids to choose from that are available throughout the United States.

## The type of potting material

Potting materials vary dramatically in terms of the amount of water they retain. For instance, sphagnum moss, a highly water-absorbent plant that is harvested from bogs to be used as a potting material, usually stays wet much longer than bark, which isn't as water-retentive.

If you're using a potting material that absorbs a lot of water, you'll want to water less often than if you use a potting material that doesn't absorb the water. To determine whether the potting material is absorbent, soak some of it in water for a few hours. Then remove the material and squeeze it. If it's absorbent, it will release this water, under pressure, like a sponge.

## The age of the potting material

Fresh potting material requires much more frequent watering for the first few weeks, until it gets properly wetted. As it gets older, it retains water longer.

## Whether the orchid is pot-bound

An overgrown orchid (sometimes referred to as an orchid that is *pot-bound*) will dry off much more quickly than one that has plenty of space in the pot. When pot space is limited, there is less potting material to hold onto the water, so the overgrown plant quickly uses it up.

In general, most orchids need to be repotted every one to two years. In Chapter 7, I give you the complete scoop on repotting orchids.

## The growing environment

Are you growing your orchids in high humidity or low? Orchids and potting materials in low humidity dry off more quickly, because the drier air quickly absorbs the moisture from both the plant and the potting material.

## The temperature

Warmer temperatures increase water evaporation because warmer air absorbs more moisture and because the plants are growing more quickly in warmer temperatures and require more water. If you're growing orchids in a cooler temperature, you won't need to water as often.

## The amount of ventilation

The more ventilation your orchids get — especially if air is vented to the outside, or if the air is hot and dry, as is found in most centrally heated homes — the quicker the water in the potting material evaporates. Gentle air movement is ideal. It will keep the air fresh without excessively drying out the plants or potting material.

## Whether the orchids are growing or dormant

When species of certain orchids (like some of the dendrobiums and catasetums) are going through their winter rest period, they need and should only be given very little water. But when they start active growth in the spring and summer, they require copious amounts of water.

In Part III, I give you information about rest requirements for specific orchids.

### The type of orchid

Some orchids, like cattleyas, like to dry out between waterings; others, like paphiopedilums, phalaenopsis, and miltonias, prefer to always be damp. This difference has a lot to do with where the particular type of orchid grows naturally. If the orchid naturally grows in an area where it doesn't get natural rainfall on a regular basis, it won't need watering as often as orchids that grow in areas of frequent rainfall.

See Part III for specific watering needs for each type of orchid.

## Proven Watering Techniques

When you've considered the factors such as potting material, environment, and type of orchid (see the preceding section), you need to make the decision as to when and how much to water.

I find the pot-weighting method of determining when to water is one of the easiest. In this method, you're relying on feel instead of precise weights. Here's what you do:

1. **Thoroughly water the orchid in its pot.**

2. **"Weigh" the pot by picking it up.**

   Now you know how heavy it is when it's saturated with water.

3. **Wait a day or so and "weigh" it again by picking it up.**

   You'll feel the difference in the weight as the potting material becomes drier.

4. **Repeat Step 3 each day until you judge, by looking at the surface and sticking your finger into the top 1 inch (2.5 cm) or so of the potting material to see if it's damp, that it's time to water.**

   Keep in mind whether this type of orchid prefers to be on the damp or dry side.

5. **Note what this dry "weight" is.**

   Now the orchid is ready to be watered thoroughly.

This entire process may sound tedious, but you'll be amazed at how quickly you catch on. And when you do, you'll always know the right time to water. Just lift the pot, note its weight, and you'll have your answer.

If you're still not quite sure about watering, keep the following watering tips in mind:

- **Grow orchids of the same type, media, pot type, and size in the same area.** This strategy will make watering them easier, because they'll have very similar moisture requirements.

- **Water with warm water.** Very cold water can cause root and bud shock, which sets back the plant and slows down its growth.

- **Always use a *water breaker* (a water diffuser that you attach to the front of your hose to soften the flow of water).** For only a few orchids, a sprinkling can with a long spout with a *rose* (a water diffuser placed on the end of the water-can spout) that has many small holes works well. These devices allow thorough watering without washing out the potting material.

  A huge selection of watering wands is available. I really like the ones with multiple settings on the head that allow you to drench or mist without changing attachments. Regulating the flow of water is much easier with wands equipped with finger triggers than it is with those that have an on-and-off valve. (See Chapter 3 for more information on tools and supplies.)

- **Never let the water breaker or end of the hose touch the ground or floor.** This commandment was given to me by my first horticulture professor, Dr. D. C. Kiplinger, who preached that floors and soil are where the diseases and insects hang out, and a hose can be an all-too-effective way of spreading them.

- **When you water, water thoroughly.** The water should pour out from the bottom of the pot. This method of watering ensures that the potting material is saturated and flushes out any excessive fertilizer salts.

- **Never let the pots of orchids sit in water for over a few hours.** If the orchid pots have saucers, make sure to keep them free of water. Excess standing water will prematurely rot the media and roots and will be a source of accumulating fertilizer salts and *pathogens* (disease-causing organisms, like bacteria, fungi, or viruses).

- **Water the orchids early in the day or afternoon.** That way, the foliage will have plenty of time to dry off before nightfall. Wet foliage in the evening is an invitation for disease.

# Over- or Underwatering: Roots Tell the Story

Over- and underwatering show many of the same symptoms because the effect of both practices is the same — damaged or destroyed root systems, which result in the orchid becoming dehydrated. The signs of dehydration include

- Pleated leaves on orchids like miltonias (see Figure 6-1)

- Excessively shriveled *pseudobulbs* (thickened, swollen stems) of some orchids, like cattleyas

- Droopy, soft, and puckered leaves on cattleyas

- Yellow and wilted bottom leaves on phalaenopsis

- *Bud blast* (in which the buds fall off instead of opening) on all orchids

**Figure 6-1:** The pleated or puckered leaf of this miltonia orchid is a sign that the orchid is dehydrated.

## Figuring out whether watering is the problem

In order to better evaluate whether over- or underwatering has caused these symptoms, remove the orchid from its pot. Many beginner growers are reluctant to do this, but if you're careful, removing the orchid from its pot won't disturb most orchids to any degree and it's an absolutely necessary procedure to see what's going on with the root system.

To determine if you've under- or overwatered your orchid, follow these steps:

1. **Turn the orchid plant, in its pot, upside-down.**

2. **Gently rap a hard object (like the handle of a gardening tool) against the pot to loosen the potting material.**

   Cup your hand over the surface of the pot to hold the loosened potting material as it falls out. Doing this over a workbench or a table covered with clean newspaper to hold the potting material is a nice, neat approach.

3. **If the potting material doesn't loosen easily, use a thin knife to circle the inside of the pot to loosen the potting material from the wall of the pot.**

   In some situations, the potting material may be so packed into the pot that it won't come out easily.

4. **When the orchid is removed from the pot, check out the potting material.**

   Is it soggy? Does it have a bad (rotting) smell? Are the roots dark and mushy? These are all signs of overwatering.

   If the roots are dry and shriveled, not stiff and plump, and have no or few growing root tips, the orchid probably hasn't gotten enough water. The potting material may be too coarse, making poor contact with the roots; otherwise, you simply haven't watered the orchid frequently enough.

5. **If the roots look okay or only slightly damaged, pot up the orchid again in fresh potting material.**

   See Chapter 7 for more details on potting orchids.

6. **If you find that the roots are badly damaged, read the following section for more information.**

## Mission: Orchid rescue and resuscitation

The approach you take to remedy root damage depends on how dire the situation is.

If the orchid still has some healthy, firm roots, cut off all the soft, mushy roots with a sterile tool, like a single-edged razor, and repot the orchid in new potting material. Go light on the watering for a few weeks to encourage new root development. Using a spray bottle, mist the orchids a few times a day to prevent the leaves from drying out.

If the roots are almost all gone, emergency measures are called for and recovery is not definite. This is what I recommend:

1. **Cut off all the dead or damaged roots.**

2. **Drench the roots with a liquid rooting hormone like Dip 'n Grow.**

3. **Let this liquid hormone dry on the roots for about an hour, then repot the orchid in fresh potting material that has been predampened.**

4. **Don't water for a day.**

5. **Water once, and then put the potted orchid in an enclosed terrarium (like a *high-top propagator,* a clear plastic box with vents at the top and a tray below to hold potting material) or an empty aquarium, with damp sphagnum moss or pebbles on the bottom to add humidity.**

6. **Close the top of the terrarium and put it in a location with diffused light.**

   In a greenhouse, this would be a shady spot with no direct sunlight. Under florescent lights, put the terrarium at the ends of the tubes where there is less illumination. If the terrarium is in the cool part of the greenhouse or growing area, put the entire terrarium on water-resistant soil or seedling heating mats, available at most garden centers. Get one that has a built-in thermostat set for about 70°F (21°C) to provide bottom heat to stimulate rooting.

7. **If you're concerned about disease, spray the orchid leaves with a disinfectant solution.**

   A good disinfectant is Physan, a commonly used hospital disinfectant available from mail-order orchid-supply companies or at garden centers.

In this environment of 100 percent humidity, the leaves won't dehydrate, so there will be no stress on the orchid while it reroots itself. Water the potting material only when it gets dry, keep the gravel or moss in the bottom of the terrarium damp, and leave the orchid enclosed until new root growth is very apparent. This may take a few months.

This method has no guarantees, but following this procedure has saved orchids for me that were in the "hopeless" category.

Figure 6-2 shows my orchid rescue, the place where I put orchids that have suffered a loss of roots. It's like a miniature greenhouse with high humidity, which encourages the orchids to form new roots.

**Figure 6-2:** My orchid rescue, the place where I put orchids that have suffered a loss of roots.

# Fertilizers: Not Magic Potions

Many people place much too much faith in fertilizers. They think fertilizer is some type of elixir that will save the day. Actually, if the orchid is in poor health, fertilizers are rarely the answer.

In fact, if the roots are damaged (a frequent problem), applying fertilizers will make the problem worse. If roots aren't functioning well, they can't absorb the fertilizer, and if the fertilizer isn't used by the orchid, it can accumulate in the orchid potting material. This buildup of fertilizer salts can further dehydrate and damage the remaining roots.

Fertilizers are most useful as a boost to help an already healthy orchid grow better.

Many people mistakenly think of fertilizer as food — which it isn't. Plants produce their own food from sunlight, carbon dioxide, and water. That's the miracle called *photosynthesis*. By fertilizing, you're merely providing minerals that your orchids can use to make photosynthesis more efficient.

The number and types of fertilizers on the market can make your head spin! You'll hear a lot of mumbo-jumbo about why one fertilizer is better than another. Fortunately, the choice is not nearly as complicated as some manufacturers seem to make it.

## What to look for in orchid fertilizers

From my experience and after listening to other veteran orchid growers, I've come to some conclusions about fertilizers. The following suggestions apply to most orchid-growing situations:

- ✔ **Look at the label and choose a fertilizer that has the words** *nitrate nitrogen* **or** *ammoniacal nitrogen,* **not** *urea.* Although all forms can be used by plants, recent research shows that the nitrate and ammoniacal forms, not urea, are most beneficial to orchids. These chemical terms may sound like Greek to you, but it's not really important for you to know any more than to look for these types of nitrogen in your fertilizer. It will be spelled out on the label.

- ✔ **Look for a fertilizer with 20 percent or less nitrogen (this is listed on the label).** High amounts of nitrogen, much more than 20 percent, are not necessary to grow the best orchids no matter what media they are grown in. Too much of any nutrient cannot be used by the orchid plant and, as a result, merely ends up as a pollutant.

- ✔ **Don't worry about the amount of phosphorus in the fertilizer.** It was earlier thought that a high-phosphorus fertilizer was necessary for better orchid bloom. This has now been found not to be the case.

- ✔ **In most cases, a fertilizer with supplementary calcium (up to 15 percent) and magnesium (up to 8 percent) is a real plus.**

- ✔ **For most water sources, adding** *trace elements* **(chemicals in very small amounts), including sodium, manganese, copper, zinc, boron, iron, and molybdenum, has been found to be beneficial to orchid growth.** Don't worry about the exact amounts; just check the fertilizer container or label to see if they appear in small amounts.

Any fertilizer that meets these requirements will do. To find out if your chosen fertilizer does, carefully look at the fertilizer container. By law, the manufacturer is required to list what chemicals are included in the fertilizer. Figure 6-3 is an example of a label so you can see what to look for.

## Interpreting the Orchid Fertilizer Label

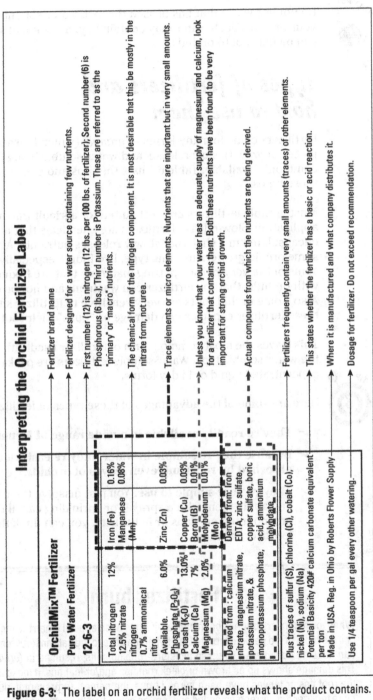

**OrchidMix™ Fertilizer** → Fertilizer brand name

**Pure Water Fertilizer** → Fertilizer designed for a water source containing few nutrients.

**12-6-3** → First number (12) is nitrogen (12 lbs. per 100 lbs. of fertilizer); Second number (6) is Phosphorous (6 lbs.); Third number is Potassium. These are referred to as the "primary" or "macro" nutrients.

| | | |
|---|---|---|
| Total nitrogen | 12% | |
| 12.5% nitrate nitrogen | | |
| 0.7% ammoniacal nitro. | | |
| Available. | 6.0% | |
| Phosphate (P₂O₅) | 13.0% | |
| Potash (K₂O) | 7% | |
| Calcuim (Ca) | 2.0% | |
| Magnesium (Mg) | | |

→ The chemical form of the nitrogen component. It is most desirable that this be mostly in the nitrate form, not urea.

| | |
|---|---|
| Iron (Fe) | 0.16% |
| Manganese (Mn) | 0.08% |
| Zinc (Zn) | 0.03% |
| Copper (Cu) | 0.03% |
| Boron (B) | 0.01% |
| Molybdenum (Mo) | 0.01% |

→ Trace elements or micro elements. Nutrients that are important but in very small amounts.

→ Unless you know that your water has an adequate supply of magnesium and calcium, look for a fertilizer that contains them. Both these nutrients have been found to be very important for strong orchid growth.

**Derived from: Iron EDTA, zinc sulfate, copper sulfate, boric acid, ammonium molybdate**

Derived from : calcium nitrate, magnesium nitrate, potassium nitrate, & monopotassium phosphate, → Actual compounds from which the nutrients are being derived.

**Plus traces of sulfur (S), chlorine (Cl), cobalt (Co), nickel (Ni), sodium (Na)** → Fertilizers frequently contain very small amounts (traces) of other elements.

**Potential Basicity 420# calcium carbonate equivalent per ton** → This states whether the fertilizer has a basic or acid reaction.

**Made in USA. Reg. in Ohio by Roberts Flower Supply** → Where it is manufactured and what company distributes it.

**Use 1/4 teaspoon per gal every other watering.** → Dosage for fertilizer. Do not exceed recommendation.

**Figure 6-3:** The label on an orchid fertilizer reveals what the product contains. Read it closely.

Do not use water that has passed through water-softening units on your orchids. Such water may contain high amounts of sodium that can be harmful to orchids.

## Types of fertilizers and how to use them

Fertilizers come in many forms — *granule* (which looks like small pieces of gravel), slow-release, and water soluble being the most commonly available. Table 6-1 lists the pros and cons of each of these types.

Most granule fertilizers are best suited for agricultural or lawn application. Slow-release fertilizers are chemicals that have been encapsulated in a shell that slowly releases nutrients. Although some orchid growers use this type, I've found, especially with some of the very porous potting materials that are frequently used with orchids, that the fertilizer can wash out and not be effective. Also, some orchid roots are very sensitive to fertilizer salts, so these fertilizer capsules can damage or "burn" their roots.

This leaves the most common form of fertilizer used with orchids — the water-soluble type. Water-soluble fertilizers are packaged as a concentrated liquid or in dry forms.

Here are some of the advantages of these types of fertilizers:

✔ **They're readily available in a wide range of formulations.**

✔ **Because they're soluble in water, they're easily and quickly absorbed by roots and even leaves of orchids.**

✔ **They're very simple to use.** You just dissolve them in water and apply them with a sprayer or sprinkling can. If the orchids are mounted on slabs or in baskets, you can dunk them in the fertilizer solution.

## Fertilizer burn

When too much fertilizer has been applied, if it has been applied when the media is dry, or if the roots of the particular orchid are hypersensitive to the salts in fertilizer, the roots can become dehydrated by these moisture-robbing salts, resulting in *fertilizer burn*. This damage shows up as brown or black root tips and/or leaf tips. It looks as though the root tips or leaves have been burned (thus, the name). To prevent it, don't apply more fertilizer than is recommended and fertilize only when the potting material is damp.

The disadvantages of water-soluble fertilizers include the following:

- ✔ **The nutrients don't last long in the potting material,** so the fertilizer needs to be applied once every two to three weeks (or constantly if you're using a very low dosage).

- ✔ **These fertilizers, in their original containers, are very concentrated and can damage the orchids if you don't dilute them correctly.**

The application rate or dosage of all fertilizers depends on the concentrations that are used. The safest procedure is to always check the fertilizer container for their recommended application rates. Never apply more than recommended or plant damage can result.

**Table 6-1     The Pros and Cons of Different Fertilizers and How to Use Them**

| Type of Fertilizer | Advantages | Disadvantages | How It Is Applied |
|---|---|---|---|
| Granule | Readily available Easy to use Inexpensive | Short-term (lasts a few to several weeks) Can easily burn orchid roots Often doesn't include valuable trace elements | In dry form On top of or incorporated into the potting material |
| Slow release | Easy to use Lasts a long time (three to nine months, depending on the formulation) | Can sometimes burn sensitive orchid roots In coarse potting material, can be washed out when watered Relatively expensive | In dry form On top of or incorporated into medium |
| Water-soluble | Readily available in a wide range of formulations Easy to apply Nutrients are instantly available for plants | Must be applied frequently — every few weeks when plants are actively growing | Diluted in water and applied by watering can |

Here are some pointers to help you know when it's time to fertilize your orchid:

✔ **Fertilizing frequently at a more dilute rate is better than fertilizing less often at a higher concentration.** Some orchid growers, including me, find that feeding their orchids every time they water with a diluted amount of fertilizer works great. It's the most natural way (as opposed to the feast-or-famine routine of fertilizing at a higher concentration every two or three weeks).

✔ **Never apply more fertilizer than is recommended by the manufacturer.** When in doubt apply less, not more, fertilizer. Remember that fertilizers are a form of salt and salts were some of the earliest weed killers, so they'll damage orchids at high concentrations.

✔ **Drench the potting material, several times in a row, every few weeks or so with fresh water that contains no nutrients to wash out any excess fertilizer salts.** This process is called *leaching.*

✔ **Look at the orchid's leaves and flowers.** Very dark green leaves that are succulent and floppy can be a sign of overfertilizing. If orchids are overfertilized, they also produce poor-quality flowers.

✔ **When the orchids are actively growing, fertilize them.** When they aren't, don't.

✔ **If the orchids are diseased and in poor condition, stop fertilizing.**

# Fertilizer deposits on pots

As water evaporates from the potting material in the pots, it leaves behind any solid minerals or salts that were dissolved in the water, including fertilizer salts. These salts can accumulate on the edges of the pots. When this salt crusting is noticed, remove it with a damp cloth. If you don't, these deposits can burn the leaves of the orchids when they touch it.

Because clay pots are porous, they tend to accumulate more salt deposits on the edges than plastic pots do. One way to prevent this is to dip the tops of the clay pots into about ½ inch of melted *paraffin* (wax used to make candles) before potting your orchids in them.

# Chapter 7

# The ABCs of Potting Materials, Containers, and Repotting

● ● ● ● ● ● ● ● ● ● ● ● ● ● ● ● ● ● ● ● ● ● ● ● ● ● ● ● ● ● ● ● ● ● ● ● ● ● ● ● ●

## *In This Chapter*

▶ Selecting the right potting materials

▶ Choosing the best container

▶ Planting an orchid in a wooden basket

▶ Repotting orchids

▶ Mounting an orchid on a slab

● ● ● ● ● ● ● ● ● ● ● ● ● ● ● ● ● ● ● ● ● ● ● ● ● ● ● ● ● ● ● ● ● ● ● ● ● ● ● ● ●

*I*f you're just starting out with orchids, the process of choosing containers and potting materials and then repotting orchids can be daunting. Orchids do have special requirements, unlike most other houseplants. But have no fear — in this chapter, I walk you through all the steps so you have the information you need. When you repot a few orchids, you'll realize that this is a very fun and rewarding part of orchid growing.

## *Choosing Potting Materials*

Just as you wouldn't be happy in any old place with four walls and a roof, your orchids won't be happy in any kind of potting material. In this section, I give you the inside scoop on what goes into potting material and which material is best for your orchid. I also give you some not-so-top-secret recipes for potting material so you can make your own — and I let you know what to do if you'd rather not.

## Knowing your potting material options

When I used the words *potting material* in the heading for this section, it wasn't just a fancy way of saying *dirt*. It's because most orchids have roots that need more air space than soil can provide. Orchids also need potting material that drains rapidly and at the same time retains moisture. Because orchids usually go at least a year, and many times longer, between repotting, they also need materials that are slow to decompose. (So if you were thinking of just throwing a little dirt in a pot and calling it a day, you'll want to think again.)

No single potting material works best for every orchid or orchid grower. In Table 7-1, I list of some of the most common potting materials used, along with some of their pros and cons.

**Table 7-1    The Pros and Cons of Various Potting Materials**

| Potting Material | Pros | Cons |
|---|---|---|
| Aliflor | Doesn't decompose | Heavy |
| | Provides good aeration | |
| Coco husk chunks | Retains moisture while also also providing sufficient air | Must be rinsed thoroughly to remove any salt residue |
| | Slower to decompose than bark | Smaller grades may retain too much moisture |
| Coco husk fiber | Retains water well | Does not drain as well as bark or coco husk chunks |
| | Decomposes slowly | |
| Fir bark | Easy to obtain | Can be difficult to wet |
| | Inexpensive | Decomposes relatively quickly |
| | Available in many *grades* (sizes) | |
| Gravel | Drains well | Heavy |
| | Inexpensive | Holds no nutrients |
| Hardwood charcoal | Very slow to decompose | Holds very little moisture |
| | Absorbs contaminants | Can be dusty to handle |

| Potting Material | Pros | Cons |
|---|---|---|
| Lava rock | Never decomposes<br><br>Drains well | Heavy |
| Osmunda fiber | Retains moisture<br><br>Slow to break down | Very expensive<br><br>Hard to find |
| Perlite (sponge rock) | Lightweight<br><br>Provides good aeration and water retention<br><br>Inexpensive | Retains too much water if used alone |
| Redwood bark | Lasts longer than fir bark | Hard to find |
| Sphagnum moss | Retains water and air<br><br>Readily available | Can retain too much water if packed tightly in the pot or after it starts to decompose |
| Styrofoam peanuts | Inexpensive<br><br>Readily available<br><br>Doesn't decompose<br><br>Rapid draining | Should not be used alone because doesn't retain water or nutrients<br><br>Best used as drainage in bottoms of pots<br><br>Can be too light for top-heavy plants |
| Tree fern fiber | Rapidly draining<br><br>Slow to decompose | Expensive<br><br>Low water retention |

# Figuring out which potting materials are best

If you read the preceding section and you're thinking, "How the heck am I supposed to choose a potting material when none of them are perfect?" don't worry. The individual potting materials are rarely used by themselves — they're usually formulated into mixtures, so the final product will retain water, drain well, and last a reasonable amount of time. Every orchid grower has his own favorite potting formulations — kind of like every grandmother has her favorite apple-pie recipe.

The combination of potting materials that will work best for your orchid depends on various factors. Answer the following questions to get an idea of what you need:

- **How often do you water?** If you tend to be heavy-handed with the sprinkling can or hose, use materials that drain well and decompose slowly.

- **What type of an orchid are you growing?** Some orchids that naturally grow on or in the ground, called *terrestrials,* usually prefer to be kept slightly damp all the time, while those that live in trees, called *epiphytes,* or grow on rocks, called *lithophytes,* want to dry off thoroughly between waterings. When you look at catalog listings or search for information on the Web about your particular orchid, look for these terms to see what growing conditions suit them best, or ask the grower you're buying from.

- **How mature are the plants?** Large plants usually do best in coarser potting materials and smaller plants do better in finer potting materials. (See the following sections for potting mixes of varying degrees of coarseness.)

- **How big are the roots of the plants?** In general, smaller roots grow better in finer, more water-retentive materials, while larger roots perform best in coarser materials.

## Psst! Getting your hands on some not-so-secret recipes

Although some orchid specialists have complicated formulations for each type of orchid they grow, I've simplified this process to two basic mixes that suit most orchids. The mixes are based on the texture or particle size of the mix, which is connected to the size of the orchid roots and their need for water retention. (If this sounds complicated, just read on — I let you know which mix works best for which orchids.)

Recommending specific potting mixes or formulations is a risky thing to do because there are so many opinions as to what works best. In truth, many different mixes will work. The most important thing is to match your watering habits to the potting material you use. If you are a heavy and frequent waterer (as most people are), use a more porous, well draining mix (like the ones I recommend in the following sections). If you tend to water less frequently, use potting mixes that contain higher percentages of some of the more water-retentive materials listed in Table 7-1.

These formulations work well for me, but you may find some other mix works better for your situation.

Keep your watering habits in mind. If your orchids tend to dry out too often, use plastic pots rather than clay and use the fine mix. If you tend to be a heavy waterer, use clay pots with the coarse mix.

### Fine mix

4 parts fine-grade fir bark *or* fine-grade coco husk chips *or* redwood bark

1 part fine charcoal

1 part horticultural-grade perlite or small-grade Aliflor

This mix works well for smaller plants of all types of orchids, slipper orchids, most oncidiums, miltonias, and any other orchids with small roots that like to stay on the damp side.

### Medium mix

4 parts medium-grade fir bark *or* medium-grade coco husk chunks

1 part medium charcoal

1 part horticultural-grade perlite or medium-grade Aliflor

This is your middle-of-the-road mix. If you aren't sure which mix to use, try this one. This mix is also good for cattleyas, phalaenopsis, and most mature orchids.

## If mixing your own is not your thing

If you'd rather just buy your mix ready-made, potting mixes are readily available from most places that sell orchids, including home-improvement stores. The mixes that they sell are very similar to the ones I outline in the preceding section. Most contain fir bark, perlite, charcoal, and sometimes some peat moss and are suitable for most orchids.

## Getting your potting material ready to use

Whatever potting material or mix you choose — whether you mix it yourself or buy it ready-made — it must be wetted before you use it. Otherwise, it will never hold moisture properly and will always dry out. Here's how you do it:

1. **Pour the amount of potting material you intend to use into a bucket that has about twice the volume of the mix.**

2. **Fill the bucket with hot water.**

   Hot water penetrates the material better than cold water.

3. **Let it soak overnight.**

4. **The next day, pour out the mix into a colander or strainer.**

5. **Rinse the mix thoroughly to wash out the dust that was in the mix.**

Now the mix is ready to use.

# Giving Your Orchids a Home: Potting Containers

Many different containers are on the market — some are more ornamental, while others have functional differences (see Figure 7-1). The most common container is the basic pot — plastic or clay.

The big differences between standard garden pots and those used for orchids are the number and size of drainage holes in the container. Orchid pots have larger holes and more of them, both in the bottom and sides of the pot, to ensure better drainage. Some are shallow and shorter than standard garden pots, with a larger base — especially useful for top-heavy orchids.

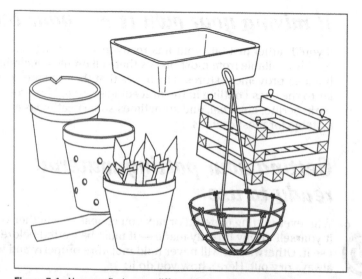

**Figure 7-1:** You can find many different types of containers for growing orchids.

You can also plant orchids in wooden baskets, usually constructed of teak or some other rot-resistant wood (see Figure 7-2).

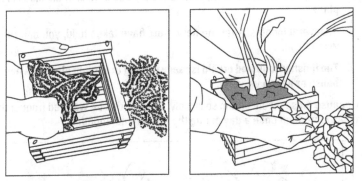

**Figure 7-2:** When potting in a basket, line the basket with sheet moss, then add standard potting mix.

# Repotting Orchids without Fear

Most beginning orchid growers are afraid to repot their orchids. Despite their reputation, orchids are tough. After all, they were first brought over from the tropics to Europe in the holds of ships and, miraculously, many of them made it alive!

In this section, I give you all the information you need to repot your orchids with confidence.

## Mounting orchids

Many orchids that are found naturally growing in trees can be mounted, instead of placed in pots. Mounting gives them perfect drainage, simulates their natural habitat, and can be an easy way to maintain them.

To mount your orchid, follow these steps (and refer to the nearby figure):

1. **Place the plant on a small handful of moistened, squeeze-dried sphagnum moss.**

2. **Spread the roots around the sphagnum moss.**

3. **Place the orchid on the mount so its center points down.**

   Don't position the orchid with the growing point up. If you do, it will collect water in the center of the plant, which can lead to disease that causes the center and growing point of the plant to rot (and can lead to death).

*(continued)*

*(continued)*

4. **After the orchid is centered properly, wrap either stainless-steel wire or clear fishing line (monofilament) around the top and bottom of the moss to hold it in place.**

   In several months, after the new roots have taken hold, you can remove the wire or line.

5. **The finished mounted orchid is ready to hang in a bright place in a home green-house or near a window.**

Because these mounts drain so rapidly, they need to be watered frequently, some-times more than once a day during the hot summer months.

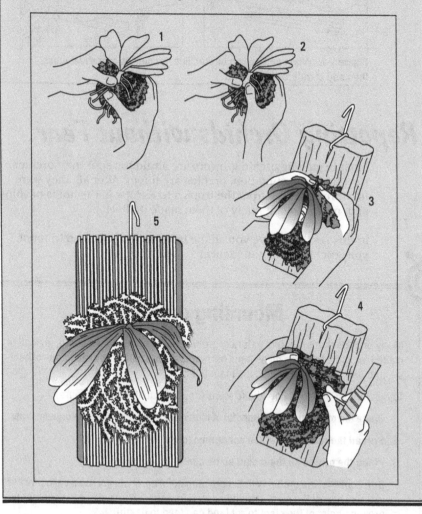

## *Knowing when you should repot*

Your orchid will tell you when it's the right time to repot. No, the plant won't speak to you (if it does, be afraid — be very, very afraid).

Here are the situations in which you'll want to repot your orchid:

- ✔ When the orchid roots are overflowing the pot
- ✔ When the plant itself is going over the edge of the pot
- ✔ When the potting material is getting soggy and drains poorly

The ideal time to repot most orchids is when the plant starts new growth, usually right after it flowers. With certain orchids like the cattleyas, you'll see a swelling at the base of the plant, which is the beginning of the new lead or shoot that will form the next stem, leaf, and flowers (see Figure 7-3). This is when orchids are putting out new roots.

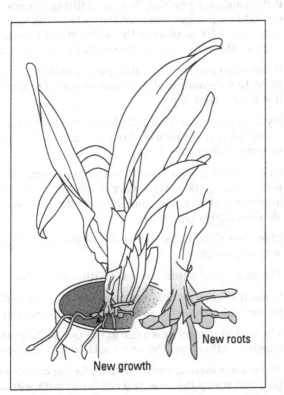

New roots

New growth

**Figure 7-3:** Cattleyas should be repotted after flowering when the new roots are about 1 inch (2.5 cm) long, the new lead growth is just appearing, and the growth of the plant has reached the edge of the pot.

If you don't repot your orchid at this new-growth stage, the new roots and growths are easily exposed to breakage and the new roots won't have any potting material to grow into and, therefore, will be more likely to dry out. If the orchid plant becomes too overgrown, you'll have trouble transplanting it later without damaging it.

## Orchid potting — step by step

Now that you know this is the right time to repot your orchid, here are the simple steps to follow (see Figure 7-4):

1. **Remove the orchid from the pot.**

   You may need to use a knife to circle the inside of the pot and loosen the roots.

2. **Remove the old, loose, rotted potting material and any soft, damaged, or dead roots.**

3. **If the roots are healthy, firm, and filling the pot, put the orchid in a pot just one size larger than the one you removed it from, placing the older growth toward the back so the new lead or growth has plenty of room.**

   **If the roots are rotted and in poor condition, repot the plant in a container of the same or one size smaller than it was removed from.**

   If you place a poorly rooted plant in too large of a container, the growing material will stay too damp, which will result in more of the roots rotting.

   Some orchid growers like to add a coarse material like broken clay pots or Styrofoam in the bottom of the pots to improve drainage. You don't have to do this if you're using shallow, azalea-type pots.

4. **Place the plant in the pot so it's at the same depth as it was originally.**

   The new shoot should be level with the pot rim.

5. **Press the fresh potting material into the pot and around the orchid roots with your thumbs and forefingers.**

   The orchid should be secure in the pot so it doesn't wiggle — otherwise, the new roots won't form properly.

6. **Place a wooden or bamboo stake in the center of the pot, and tie up the new and old leads with soft string or twist ties.**

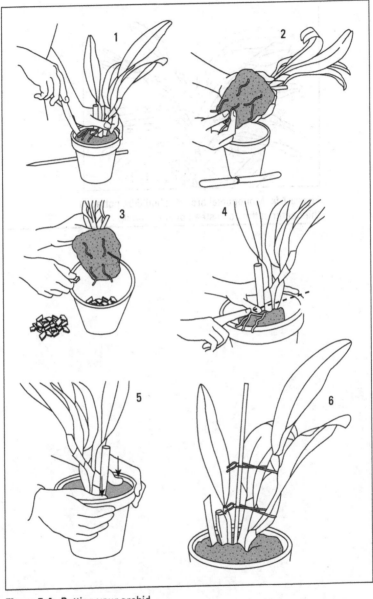

**Figure 7-4:** Potting your orchid.

*Monopodial* orchids are those with one growing point that always grows vertically, not sideways (such as phalaenopsis, angraecums, and vandas), as shown in Figure 7-5. The potting process for these orchids is very similar to the cattleya process (outlined in the preceding steps), except that the orchid should be placed in the *center* of the container, rather that toward the back.

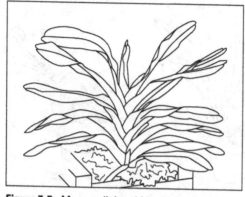

**Figure 7-5:** Monopodial orchids should be potted in the center of the pot instead of at the back.

# Chapter 8

# Two, Four, Six, Eight, Let Your Orchids Propagate: Multiplying Your Orchids

**In This Chapter**

▶ Making more orchids by dividing them

▶ Separating babies from their parents

▶ Making more orchids from cuttings

▶ Producing plants from back bulbs

*B*ecause orchids are slower growing than most other plants, the process of multiplying them takes more time. To rear an orchid from seed to bloom can take as long as five to seven years! The other methods I show you in this chapter are much quicker, but they're still not as speedy as reproducing common garden plants. Multiplying your orchids is worth the effort, however, because orchids are valuable plants that will keep growing forever.

## Dividing Your Orchids

Dividing orchids is the surest and swiftest way to increase your orchids. This method only works with *sympodial-type* orchids (ones that grow sideways across the top of the pot like cattleya, shown in Figure 8-1). Just about all the orchids in this book — except for those in Chapter 10 — are sympodials.

For the cattleya types, you want to have divisions of at least three or four growths (called *pseudobulbs*). For other types, you can divide them with fewer growths, but for best results, the larger the divisions the better.

You may want to divide your orchid because

- ✔ **The plant has grown too big to handle.**

- ✔ **You want to share or trade a piece of the orchid you have with another plant lover.**

- ✔ **The *rhizomes* (creeping stems of the orchid) are growing over each other in a tangled mess.**

When cutting the orchid plant, use a very sharp knife or pruners that have been sterilized to prevent disease spread. After you've divided the plant, turn to Chapter 7 for information on potting it.

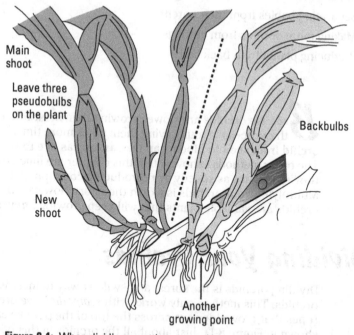

**Figure 8-1:** When dividing a cattleya, try to have at least three, if not four, front growths.

Do not divide your orchids when they're too small or when they don't have enough growths. The largest divisions with the most pseudobulbs will grow quickest to blooming plants. You'll always get the best blooming from your orchids when they have multiple divisions or growths.

Dividing a large orchid with many growths can be confusing. Make a drawing of the plant growth pattern on a sheet of paper, and mark where you'll make your cuts before you start doing it, as shown in Figure 8-2.

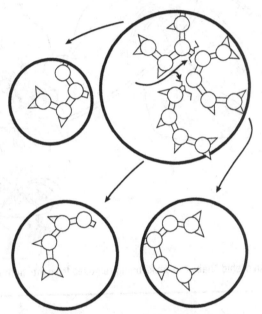

**Figure 8-2:** Making a drawing showing how a large orchid will be divided helps simplify the process.

# Giving Babies a New Home

The Hawaiian name for baby is *keiki*. Interestingly, the orchid crowd adopted this name to refer to a baby plant, especially one that sprouts on the stem of a mature orchid.

Some plants, like the phalaenopsis, sometimes produce babies on the flower stem (see Figure 8-3). When this happens, leave these young plants on the flower stem until they've developed several roots a few inches long. Then you can cut the young plant from the flower stem and pot it following the guidelines in Chapter 7.

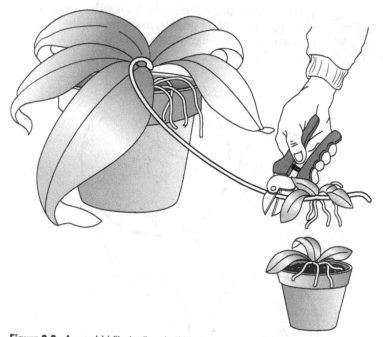

**Figure 8-3:** An orchid "baby," or *keiki,* being removed from the mother plant and then potted.

When an orchid grows very tall and has extending roots from its stem, you can create more plants by cutting out the top several inches of the orchid stem that contains the roots and potting it (this is known as *topping* an orchid). The bottom half of the plant will then usually form baby plants that will sprout along the stem. These babies can eventually be cut off and planted. Figure 8-4 illustrates the three steps of topping an orchid:

1. **Remove the top portion of the stem, allowing ample roots.**

2. **Pot the portion you've just removed.**

3. **Leave the mother plant in its original container and wait for the baby plants to sprout from its stem.**

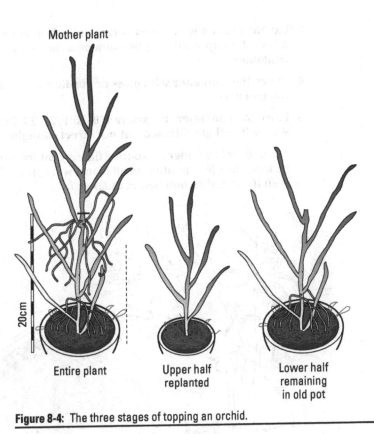

Mother plant

20cm

Entire plant

Upper half
replanted

Lower half
remaining
in old pot

**Figure 8-4:** The three stages of topping an orchid.

# Producing New Plants from Cuttings

Some orchids have *canes,* or long stems, that you can cut up into pieces called *cuttings*. Here's how this works (see Figure 8-5):

1. **Cut off one of the long stems or canes with sharp, clean pruners.**

2. **With a sharp, sterile knife, cut sections of the cane so that each section contains at least two *nodes* (the regions of the stems where the leaves used to be attached).**

   Nodes are marked by circular scars around the stems.

3. **Lay the cut stems or canes horizontally, half-buried, on a bed of damp sand or sphagnum moss in a shallow container.**

4. **Cover the container with glass or plastic wrap to hold in the moisture.**

5. **Place the container in a warm (70–75°F/21–24°C) area where it will get diffused but not direct sunlight.**

   About 6 inches under a two-tube fluorescent fixture would be ideal. In a few months, small plants will sprout. They can then be potted as outlined in Chapter 7.

**Figure 8-5:** Producing more orchids from stem or cane cuttings.

# Growing Orchids from Back Bulbs

After some types of orchids, like cymbidiums and oncidiums, bloom, their older stems, called *backbulbs,* eventually lose their leaves and become lifeless looking. If you leave them in the pot, they probably won't ever produce new growth. If, however, you remove them from the main plant and handle them in a special manner, they can produce new young plants.

Here are the steps to follow (see Figure 8-6):

1. Cut off from the mother plant the older back bulbs that no longer have leaves.

2. Put a 2-inch (5-cm) layer of damp sphagnum moss in a plastic bag.

3. Place several of the backbulbs with their bottoms about one-fourth buried in sphagnum moss in the plastic bag and seal it.

   Put this bag in a warm (70–75°F/21–24°C) spot that receives bright diffused light, not direct sunlight. In about two months, you should start to see some new growth.

4. When the leaves are a few inches long, place the young plants as a group in a shallow container in diffused light.

   Let them grow for several months. Then transplant them into their own pots.

**Figure 8-6:** Growing new orchids from backbulbs.

# Growing orchids from seeds: Leave it to the pros

Raising orchids from seeds is not a simple task. In fact, it's quite complicated — and it wasn't until the 1920s that the professionals figured it out. The biggest problem is that the orchid seeds are *naked,* which means they don't have their own food source like most other plants. As a result, to successfully grow them, you have to provide them with a nutrient solution along with a special fungus that makes this food available to them.

All this is done in laboratory flasks. The seed is incredibly small — one seed can weight as little as 35 millionths of an ounce! They're so small that a seed pod a few inches across can hold over 100,000 seeds.

Growing orchids from seeds is not something recommended for beginners. Leave raising orchids from seeds to the experts.

If you're really interested in growing orchids from seeds, you can try a compromise: Get small plants that have already grown for a year or more in shallow containers outside of a lab environment (see the figure). This is a fun and inexpensive way to have some extra orchids to trade or give to friends. If you're new to this, start with fast-growing types like phalaenopsis. If you're lucky, you'll see blooms in a few years.

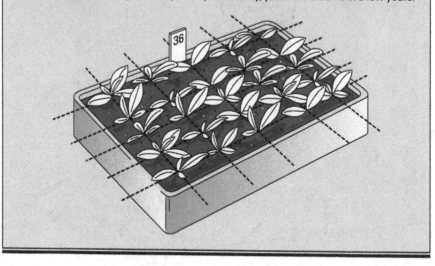

# Chapter 9

# Keeping Your Orchids Pest- and Disease-Free

*A*lthough orchids are relatively pest-free plants, if you have them long enough, you'll eventually have to deal with an invasion of some bug or disease. Fortunately, there aren't many pests to contend with and they aren't that difficult to identify. In this chapter, I stress the safest and most effective ways to control these problems.

Always start with the least toxic solution. If you are careful and inspect your orchids on a regular basis and detect the problems before they progress too far, you will rarely have to resort to more poisonous materials. The more poisonous materials should be your last line of defense.

# *Preventing Problems Before They Start*

Most insect and disease problems can be prevented by good plant sanitation. Here are some steps to take to prevent pest problems from getting out of hand:

- ✔ **Always sterilize your cutting tools.** See the nearby sidebar, "How to sterilize your tools," for more information.

- ✔ **Make a practice of regularly inspecting the tips of new growth and the undersides of the leaves.** This is where most bugs hang out.

- ✔ **Provide the best growing conditions possible.** When orchids are under stress, they're more susceptible to disease and insect infestations.

- ✔ **When repotting, always use new or cleaned and sterilized pots.**

- ✔ **Buy plants that are clean and healthy.** Beware of the "bargain" or leftover plants; many have serious problems. Unless they're in excellent condition, stay away from them.

- ✔ **Don't allow weeds to infest your pots of orchids.** They can harbor insects.

- ✔ **Keep the floor or ground in your growing area free of weeds, dead leaves, and dead flowers.**

## How to sterilize your tools

These are the two methods that I use for sterilization:

- ✔ **Chemical sterilization:** Dilute household bleach — one part bleach to nine parts water. Soak your tools in them for a few minutes before you use them. Most chemicals that are used to sterilize tools, like bleach, are highly corrosive, so after you've sterilized these tools, be sure to thoroughly rinse them with clean water or their metal will quickly rust.

- ✔ **Heat sterilization:** This is a very fast and clean way to sterilize tools. You can use a compact propane torch for this, but I've found the most convenient way is to use a small butane hand torch (see Chapter 3) like the ones sold to make the crust of crème brûlée. With these torches, you merely flame the tool on the cutting edges until they get red. Let the tool cool, and it's ready to use.

## Orchid euthanasia

Sometimes the best solution is to dispose of a sickly orchid. If you've tried the preventative and curative measures outlined in this chapter and still the orchid doesn't seem to be recovering, getting rid of it is the best solution. When a plant becomes too weakened by infection or a bad infestation of insects, it isn't likely to recover — and while you're hoping this will happen, the infested plant can spread its problem to your other healthy orchids. So bite the bullet and bury it in your trash can!

Always isolate new orchids from your other plants for four to six weeks. During this time, scrutinize them for any signs of insects.

# Besting the Bugs

The most important aspect of pest control is vigilance. Frequently, people say, "I don't know where these bugs came from! All of a sudden my orchid was infested with them!" Well, I'm here to tell you that this isn't the way it happens. Even though most insects do reproduce faster than rabbits, infestations don't happen overnight.

Things can get out of hand quickly, though, if you don't make a point of closely inspecting your orchids regularly. Keep on the lookout, because if you can detect the pests when they're in small numbers, getting rid of them will be much easier.

Many of the pests described in this chapter, like mites and thrips, are very tiny, so they're difficult to see with the naked eye. Buy yourself a 10x hand lens at a camera shop. It'll make the task much easier.

## Identifying common orchid pests

When you first notice pests, you need to promptly and properly identify them so you can be sure to apply the most effective control. In the following sections, I describe the common orchid pests. Later in the chapter, I tell you what to do if your orchid has them.

In many cases, especially if there are many pests present, you'll have to apply control measures repeatedly, every seven to ten days, at least three times. This is because these creatures have laid eggs that are resistant to the control measure and hatch later. By repeating the control several times, you'll kill these next generations of pests after they emerge from their eggs.

### Aphids

These are probably the most ubiquitous insect pests of them all. They come in all colors — including green, red, pink, black, and yellow — and they're usually found on the new, succulent growth including the flower buds (see Figure 9-1). They feed with syringe-like mouth parts and are particularly damaging to buds by causing them to be deformed when they open. Aphids are also very effective carriers of disease, especially viruses.

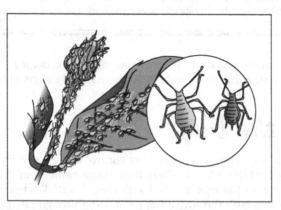

**Figure 9-1:** Aphids are usually found in clusters on flower buds and young shoots and leaves.

 If you see clear sticky droplets anywhere on you plant, look out for aphids. This material, euphemistically called *honey dew,* is actually aphid waste. This sticky substance can also be excreted by any other piercing/sucking insect, such as scale.

### Mealybugs

The name of this creature pretty much describes what this insect looks like — mealy or cottony masses (see Figure 9-2). It's found in similar areas as aphids — the growing tips, buds, and flower stems. One type is also found on the roots. This is a bothersome pest that usually needs multiple insecticide treatments to get rid of it.

### Thrips

Thrips can be very destructive, especially to flower buds, maturing flowers, and young leaves. They are miniscule buggers that look something like long gnats and are very difficult to see with the naked eye. Their damage is easier to detect — it shows up as light streaks on the flowers or stippling on the leaves. The flower buds are also usually deformed.

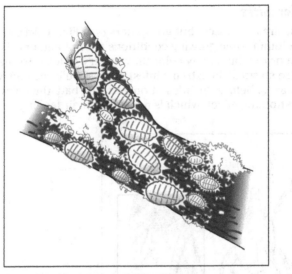

**Figure 9-2:** Mealybugs look like white cottony masses.

## Scale

This is another creature that comes in various forms, but most have a shell that serves as a type of armor for the soft insect body that is protected by it (see Figure 9-3). This shell must be penetrated by a chemical or by rubbing it off before you can kill the insect. They're frequently found on the undersides of the leaves near the middle vein of the leaf or on the edges of the leaf. They also commonly hang out on the flower stems. This is a very difficult insect to totally eradicate, but with persistence, it can effectively be controlled.

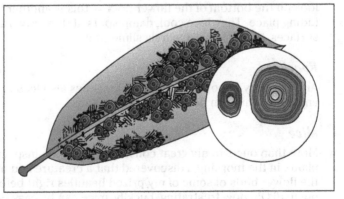

**Figure 9-3:** Scale is a very common pest on orchids.

### Spider mites

These are not insects but are spiders (see Figure 9-4). They're often found when growing conditions are hot and dry. They can be green or red, but in any color they're very difficult to see because they're so small. In extreme infestations, you'll see fine webbing on the leaves. Before the infestation gets this bad, the foliage will take on a stippling effect, which is a result of their feeding.

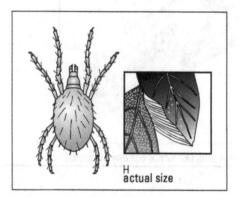

H
actual size

**Figure 9-4:** Spider mites are very small, hard-to-see pests that can be very destructive.

### Slugs and snails

Snails and slugs (see Figure 9-5) head most people's list as being one of the most revolting of all orchid pests. They can do extensive damage to young orchid roots and stems and developing and maturing flowers. They usually come out at night, so if you suspect them, take a flashlight in the evening to search for these culprits. Also, look on the bottom of the flower pots — this is another favorite hiding place. They love cool, damp spots. If they travel across dry surfaces, they'll leave a telltale slime trail.

### Roaches

Another very unpopular beast, cockroaches also feed at night and enjoy munching on flowers and flower buds.

### Mice

More than once, to my great consternation, upon inspecting my plants in the morning, I discovered that a creature had nibbled off the flower buds of some of my prized beauties right before they opened! Oh, how frustrating! Luckily, mice can be easy controlled.

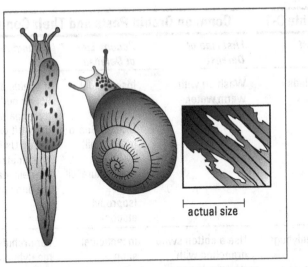

**Figure 9-5:** Snails and slugs eat holes in flowers and leaves at night.

### Bees and other pollinating insects

These are not really harmful creatures — they don't cause any physical damage to orchids, but if they land on the flowers and pollinate them, the flowers will very soon collapse. So if you want your flowers to last the longest, keep pollinating insects out of your growing area.

## Finding safe pest-control measures

Many of the chemical controls for insects and diseases can damage the plants to which they're applied if they're misused. To be on the safe side, always read the pesticide label to see if orchids are listed as a plant that this chemical should *not* be used with. And when applying the pesticide, never use more than the dosage recommended and apply it in the cool of the early morning. Also make sure that the potting material is damp — a moisture-stressed orchid is much more easily damaged by pesticides.

The pest-control methods in Table 9-1 are listed in their approximate order of safety and are readily available. Always start off with the first line of defense. Some of the least toxic solutions must be applied more frequently, because they kill on contact and aren't residual (they don't stick around after they're applied). Most don't smell bad — an important feature for homegrown plants. Some, like Orange Guard, also serve as pest repellents (which means they'll kill the pests currently there and also repel future pests).

| Table 9-1 | Common Orchid Pests and Their Controls | | |
|---|---|---|---|
| **Pest** | **First Line of Defense** | **Second Line of Defense** | **Comments** |
| Aphids | Wash off with warm water. | Insecticidal soap<br><br>Orange Guard (orange oil)<br><br>Horticultural oil<br><br>Isopropyl alcohol | If aphids are on the flower buds of orchids, try repeatedly washing them off with warm water. Using any chemical may damage the delicate developing buds or flowers. |
| Mealybugs | Use a cotton swab drenched with isopropyl alcohol. | Insecticidal soap<br><br>Horticultural oil<br><br>Neem | For orchids with mealybugs on their roots, remove the orchid from the pot, soak the roots in a solution of insecticidal soap for a few hours, then repot in a clean new pot with new potting material. |
| Thrips | Neem<br><br>Horticultural oil<br><br>Insecticidal soap | Malathion<br><br>Orthene | Malathion and Orthene are effective on a broad range of insect problems but they both reek, so be sure to apply them outside of the living area. |
| Scale | Use a cotton swab drenched with isopropyl alcohol and wipe across the armored shell of this insect. Make sure that you penetrate this shell.<br><br>Orange Guard | Insecticidal soap<br><br>Neem<br><br>Horticultural oils | This is a difficult pest to eradicate. You'll have to apply controls repeatedly to get rid of it. Before I spray, I usually try to rub off the armored shells of the scale with my fingers, then wash the leaf with mild soapy water. Then I spray with my chosen control. |

| Pest | First Line of Defense | Second Line of Defense | Comments |
|------|------------------------|-------------------------|----------|
| Spider mites | Wash off with a strong stream of warm water. | Insecticidal soap<br><br>Horticultural oils<br><br>Orthene | To prevent mite infestations, keep your orchid properly watered and in a growing area that is not too hot. |
| Snails and slugs | Old beer (The yeast in beer is a strong attractant to snails and slugs. Put out a shallow platter of beer (about ½ inch deep), and wait for these creatures to belly up to the bar at nightfall. The next day, you'll find them drowned in the brew.<br><br>Put out pieces of lettuce in the eveningthat will attract slugs and snails. This lettuce, with attached feeding slugs, can be removed and discarded in the morning. | Sluggo | If you use baits, be sure that they're harmless to pets, as Sluggo is. |
| Mice | Live traps | Old-fashioned snap traps. Peanut butter is an effective bait. | I would not recommend using poison baits. They could harm your pets, and the mice that die from this poison frequently end up in the walls of your house and the smell takes weeks to dissipate. |
| Roaches | Orange Guard | Roach aerosol sprays — use on the floor, not on plants. | Orange Guard both repels and kills roaches. And it smells good! |

If you want more technical information on orchid pests and their controls, I highly recommend the booklet published by the American Orchid Society called *Orchid Pest and Diseases*. It can be purchased online at the American Orchid Society's Orchid Emporium/ Bookstore (http://user889628.wx10.registeredsite.com/ miva/merchant.mv?Screen=PROD&Store_Code=OE&Product_ Code=S0103&Category_Code=AH).

Don't spray aerosol insect controls, such as those designed for killing ants, roaches, and wasps, on your orchid plants. These are intended to be used to kill insects outdoors and in the kitchen, but if sprayed directly on your orchid plants, they can cause serious damage.

All horticultural oils are not the same. Do not use dormant oils. Use the ones called *superior* oils. They're much thinner and more refined and are meant to be used when the plants are actively growing. One common brand name is SunSpray Ultra-Fine.

# Is There a Fungus Among Us?

Orchids are tough plants, and if you grow them in the correct cultural conditions and take the preventative measures mentioned in this chapter, they'll rarely suffer from fatal diseases. Still, being aware of what can happen when things go wrong is a good idea.

Diseases are somewhat trickier than bugs to deal with because you really can't see them. You just see the damage they leave behind — such as rotten plant centers or spots on the leaves.

The damage that most fungal and bacterial diseases leave behind are circular or oblong spots on the foliage or flowers (see Figure 9-6). Sometimes they also cause the center growing point, called the *crown,* to turn black or rot and may lead to the death of the plant. When this happens, the crown has been killed by the organism and the pattern of spots or rots is a symptom of the disease and is one of the ways that a disease is identified. Fortunately, most of the controls that I mention in this chapter are effective against a broad range of disease problems, so an exact disease diagnosis is seldom necessary to remedy the problem.

Viruses are dreaded by orchid growers because there is no practical cure for them. The most obvious symptom of a virus infection is streaking or color breaks in the flower.

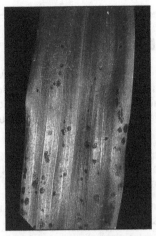

**Figure 9-6:** Leaf spots like these are usually caused by fungal organisms.

Detecting these symptoms is nearly impossible — in my 40 years of growing orchids, I've rarely been able to accurately identify a virus on my orchids. Of course, that doesn't mean my orchids didn't have some viruses that I didn't detect, but viruses aren't common, especially if you buy high-quality plants and follow the prevention methods outlined here.

Refer to the "Preventing Problems Before They Start" section, earlier in this chapter. This information pertains as much to diseases as it does to pest damage.

Here are a few other pointers that relate specifically to disease:

✓ **Water your orchids during the day when the moisture will evaporate from the leaves before nightfall.** Cool, damp leaves and water left in the crowns of the plants in the evening are an invitation to disease.

✓ **Make sure your orchids have enough airflow.** This reduces the time moisture stays on the leaves and removes stagnant air.

✓ **Remove diseased leaves with a sharp sterile knife or scissors.** (See the sidebar, "When surgery is required," later in this chapter.)

✓ **Sterilize your cutting tools each time you use them on another plant.**

✓ **When you find a disease problem, treat it right away.** Procrastinating could cost your orchid its life.

# When surgery is required

Performing surgery to cut out the infection is the simplest and most effective method of stopping the spread of disease. A single-edge razor blade is ideal for the job because it's extremely sharp and sterile and can be disposed of after the operation. The sharpness is important so that as little as possible of the healthy tissue is damaged in the process.

Remove all the damaged or diseased leaf by cutting the leaf off about ½ inch to 1 inch into healthy leaf tissue that shows no signs of the disease. Be careful not to cut into the diseased tissue and then into healthy tissue, or you'll spread the disease.

Some people dress the edge of the cut with a simple fungicidal material like sulfur or cinnamon, but this usually isn't necessary.

Here are the steps that I recommend:

1. **If the plant is badly diseased, discard it.**

   You probably won't be able to save it, and it could infect your other healthy plants.

2. **If you find dark brown spots that look like disease and they are close to the end of the leaf, remove this section of the leaf.**

   See the sidebar "When surgery is required."

3. **As a general sanitation practice, after you've performed surgery or if your orchid has a disease spot that cannot be removed surgically, spray the leaves with a mild fungicide/ bactericide and hope for the best.**

   Physan 20, Phyton 27, Natriphene, or RD-20 are all mild fungicides/bactericides that work for this purpose.

4. **Reevaluate the area you're growing the orchid in to be sure it's getting enough air circulation and you're doing all you can to follow the recommended disease-prevention measures.**

All chemical pesticides are poisons that have some toxicity to humans. Read the precautions on the pesticide label and follow them carefully. Wear rubber gloves (the disposable ones work great) when mixing and spraying these materials.

# Part III
# The Best Orchids for Rookies

The 5th Wave                    By Rich Tennant

"Chernoff, look at the fascinating formations on these orchids. Chernoff?"

## In this part . . .

*I*n this part, I give you a look at some gorgeous orchids that will love to have you take them home. With the tens of thousands of different kinds of orchids out there, the choice about which ones you should consider giving a home is daunting. Choosing the right orchid can make a big difference in your success with orchids. In this part, I show you many of the exciting possibilities. I've purposely chosen to introduce you to orchids that are easy to find and are widely adaptable to a variety of growing conditions. You can have confidence that the orchids in this part are top performers.

# Chapter 10

# Moth Orchids and Their Relatives: The Best Choice for Beginners

· · · · · · · · · · · · · · · · · · · · · · · · · · · · · · · · · · · · · · · · · · · · · · · · · ·

### In This Chapter

▶ Finding perfect starter orchids

▶ Knowing the various types of moth orchids

▶ Looking at Africa's gift to orchid lovers — the angraecoids

▶ Considering vandas and some other moth-orchid cousins

· · · · · · · · · · · · · · · · · · · · · · · · · · · · · · · · · · · · · · · · · · · · · · · · · ·

*T*his type of orchid is the most popular grown today. In fact, according to the American Orchid Society, moth orchids account for 75 percent of all orchids sold!

Moth orchids (phalaenopsis) offer everything that most orchid growers admire and are the fastest and easiest to grow. They bloom for a long period of time — from many weeks to months. The flowers are classy and borne on elegant arched sprays. And moth orchids come in a broad range of colors. Their foliage is beautiful glossy green or marbled, they have very modest light requirements, and they grow well in temperatures commonly found in the home.

Moth orchids are definitely the orchids to start with, and after you experience the great satisfaction that they provide, you may decide to stay with them. The standard pink, white, and striped ones commonly sold in the box stores and at flower shops are the essence of style, but in addition to these beauties, there are many new and exciting colors, color patterns, and growth habits that even increase their desirability. Although most phalaenopsis are not fragrant, some are.

In this chapter, I tell you all about moth orchids and their relatives.

# Mirror, Mirror on the Wall: The Beauty of Moth Orchids

Moth orchids are beautiful plants, and in this section, I fill you in on exactly what to expect from yours.

## Leaves

All the moth orchids have handsome foliage. Many of them have dark-green, leathery, glossy leaves, while others exhibit exquisitely marbled dark-green and gray-green leaves, so even when these plants aren't in bloom, they remain quite attractive (see Figure 10-1).

**Figure 10-1:** A close-up of the beautifully patterned leaf of *Phalaenopsis stuartiana*.

# Flower shapes

The various types of moth orchids have very similar shapes, though many of the newer varieties have a very rounded look. Figure 10-2 shows you the names of the parts of the moth orchid flowers. Because moth orchids epitomize style, they're frequently used in flower arrangements and in simple, yet chic, corsages.

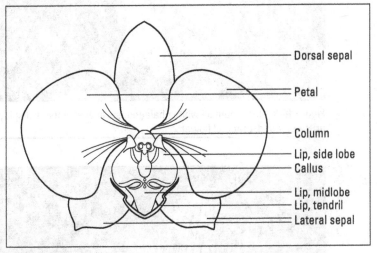

- Dorsal sepal
- Petal
- Column
- Lip, side lobe
- Callus
- Lip, midlobe
- Lip, tendril
- Lateral sepal

**Figure 10-2:** The parts of a moth orchid (phalaenopsis) flower.

# Flower colors

White, pink, and candy-striped are the "standard" moth orchids that are most commonly found at flower shops and box stores as both potted plants and cut flowers for wedding bouquets (see Figure 10-3, Figure 10-4, and the color insert). These colors of moth orchids seem to have reached the pinnacle of perfection in flower size and shape and, because of modern reproduction and growing methods, they're highly affordable. In fact, in Europe and certain large urban centers in the United States, they're commonly purchased as an expendable blooming potted plant that is discarded after its many weeks of bloom.

**Figure 10-3:** Just about all white phalaenopsis available today display pristine, round, graceful flowers.

**Figure 10-4:** Candy-striped moth orchids present a striking picture. This one is called *Phalaenopsis* Jackie Debonis.

I don't recommend any specific varieties within this group because there are so many. These types of phalaenopsis have been perfected to such a degree that just about all of them available these days would be ones you would be happy to give a home.

Due to the fine efforts of orchid hybridizers in the United States, Asia, and other parts of the world, we now have moth orchids with a huge variety of flower colors — from harlequins with random spotting patterns backed with yellow or white petals (see Figure 10-5) to dark purple, and rich pink with white lips (see Figure 10-6), clear yellows, greens, and burgundy reds,. About the only color that isn't yet found in phalaenopsis is blue, and breeders are working diligently to add this color to the palate.

To intensify the markings on these orchids, try growing them in a little drier, cooler, and brighter location than usual when they're starting to flower.

**Figure 10-5:** A harlequin-type of orchid, *Phalaenopsis* Sue Chin.

**Figure 10-6:** *Phalaenopsis* Hilo Lip is a dark cerise with a bright white lip.

# Encore! Encore! A second show

One of the great features about moth orchids is their ability to produce a secondary flower spike that branches off the main one (as shown in the nearby figure). This will make your flower show go on for months!

To make this happen, after the flowers have stopped blooming on the flower spike, feel along this bare spike and notice the bumps along this stem. These knobby structures are called *nodes*. At the base of these nodes are resting flower buds. Your mission is to wake up one of these buds so it will produce another flower spike. Notice where the first flower opened on the stem, and go to the next node down, toward the base of the plant. This is where you cut off the spent flower spike. After you do this, in most cases, this will stimulate the production of a secondary flower spike at this node.

*Remember:* Don't bloom your moth orchids to death! Sometimes moth orchids don't know what's good for them. They just keep blooming to the point of exhausting all their energy. If the orchid is a robust plant, this continual bloom is okay. But if the leaves are puckered and the plant looks worn out, or if the plant is very young and not very established, you're better off cutting off the flower spike and enjoying it in a flower arrangement. This will give the plant rest and an opportunity to put its energy into producing new roots and leaves so it will be strong enough to produce even more flowers on its next flowering.

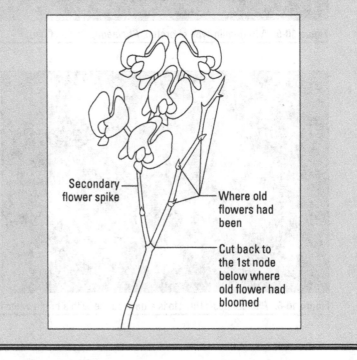

Secondary flower spike

Where old flowers had been

Cut back to the 1st node below where old flower had bloomed

## *Scents*

Few beginning orchid lovers realize that some phalaenopsis, including the one shown in Figure 10-7, are blessed with a wonderful perfume. Certain moth orchids from the wild naturally have this characteristic and, when they're used as parents, they sometimes pass this quality on to their offspring. In this section, I give you lists of some specific varieties to look for.

When you're buying other moth orchids, check to see if any of them have these plants listed as their parents; this will increase their chances of being fragrant.

**Figure 10-7:** One of the most popular of the fragrant moth orchids is *Phalaenopsis* Orchid World 'Bonnie Vasquez' AM/AOS.

Here are some of the sweet-smelling phalaenopsis hybrids that I have grown and enjoyed:

- ✔ *Phalaenopsis* **Ambo Buddha 'SW':** This is another contribution to the moth-orchid world from Taiwanese breeders. The colors on the 2½-inch (6-cm) flowers are dazzling. (See the color insert for a full-color photo.)

- ✔ *Phalaenopsis* **Caribbean Sunset 'Sweet Fragrance':** A delightful miniature with 2-inch (5-cm) rose-red flowers that has a rose fragrance. The leaves reach about 6 inches (15 cm) long.

- ✔ *Phalaenopsis* **Dottie Woodson:** Varnished, blood-red sweet-smelling 2-inch (5-cm) flowers are produced on multiple spikes borne above handsome, medium-glossy, green foliage.

- ✔ *Phalaenopsis* **Ember 'Blumen Insel' AM/AOS:** 2½-inch (6-cm) glossy, waxy, solid, dark red flowers borne on thick florescence. This flower frequently blooms more than once a year.

- ✔ *Phalaenopsis* **Kilby Cassviola 'Sweet Fragrance':** Gets its spicy fragrance from one of its parents, *Phalaenopsis violacea*. It's another compact grower with glistening white flowers about 2½ inches (6 cm) across, with light-brown barring on the lower part of the flower.

- ✔ *Phalaenopsis* **Orchid World 'Bonnie Vasquez' AM/AOS:** There are many different forms of this classic variety (refer to Figure 10-7). Most have leathery, thick, long-lasting, glossy yellow flowers brightly marked with red or maroon spots or stripes.

- ✔ *Phalaenopsis* **Perfection Is 'Chen' FCC/AOS:** One of my personal favorites because its flat, 2½-inch (6-cm) waxy, yellow flowers are brilliantly decorated with burgundy red spots and have a clove or carnation scent.

Here are some other hybrids noted for their fragrance:

- ✔ *Phalaenopsis* Sweet Memory
- ✔ *Phalaenopsis* George Vasquez 'Eureka' FCC/AOS
- ✔ *Phalaenopsis* Luedde-violacea 'Anna Red' HCC/AOS
- ✔ *Phalaenopsis* Peach State
- ✔ *Phalaenopsis* Penang Girl
- ✔ *Phalaenopsis* Princess Kaiulani
- ✔ *Phalaenopsis* Rare Vintage
- ✔ *Phalaenopsis* Tabasco Tex
- ✔ *Phalaenopsis* Valentinii
- ✔ *Phalaenopsis* Wes Addison
- ✔ *Phalaenopsis* Zuma Aussie Delight 'Zuma Canyon' AM/AOS

Some of the phalaenopsis *species* (those in the form naturally found in the wild) are fragrant and also are used in breeding to pass this characteristic to new varieties. These species are a little bit harder to find and grow but are worth the effort:

- ✔ *Phalaenopsis amboinensis:* Musky fragrance.
- ✔ *Phalaenopsis bastianii:* Very fragrant.
- ✔ *Phalaenopsis bellina:* A very fragrant scent of lily-of-the-valley and freesia. A compact grower whose flowers are borne sequentially (see Figure 10-8).

✔ ***Phalaenopsis fasciata:*** Light rosy-floral scent.

✔ ***Phalaenopsis gigantea:*** Huge leaves — they can be more than 2 feet (60 cm) long! The flowers are about 2 inches (5 cm) and smell like orange peels.

✔ ***Phalaenopsis hieroglyphica:*** White flowers with red patterns that look like hieroglyphics with a fragrance similar to a rose.

✔ ***Phalaenopsis lueddemanniana:*** Yellow to white flowers with dark mahogany spots that emit a light sweet fragrance.

✔ ***Phalaenopsis mannii:*** A Nepalese native that displays 1- to 2-inch (2.5- to 5-cm) narrow yellow flowers with dark-brown barring with a purple and white lip. Its flowers can last up to three months and have the light scent of oranges (see Figure 10-9).

✔ ***Phalaenopsis odesta:*** A summer bloomer from Borneo that has a creamy white flower with purple freckles smelling like honeysuckle or lilacs.

✔ ***Phalaenopsis schilleriana:*** An orchid with 3- to 3½-inch (8- to 9-cm) pink, lightly rose-scented flowers that can number into the hundreds on a mature plant. The dark-green foliage is handsomely marked in silver.

✔ ***Phalaenopsis tetraspis:*** Small, glossy white flowers with a strong sweet scent that are lightly marked in purple.

✔ ***Phalaenopsis violacea:*** A compact plant that is very fragrant, smelling like spice and cinnamon. The glossy green leaves are another attractive feature.

**Figure 10-8:** *Phalaenopsis bellina* has a lily-of-the-valley fragrance that permeates any room it's in.

Figure 10-9: *Phalaenopsis mannii* is quite variable in its flower color.

When it comes to moth orchid flower fragrance:

✔ Usually these orchids are fragrant during the day.

✔ On occasion, their scent will only last for a few hours each day.

✔ Sometimes the flowers have to be open for a few days before they emit a scent.

✔ Their perfume will be strongest on still, hot, sunny days.

## Size

Some of the glorious moth orchids you see in the stores make an impressive show with their 24- to 36-inch (60- to 90-cm) arcing flower spikes, but these plants may not fit in the more limited growing space you can provide. Luckily, there are diminutive moth orchids that thrive in smaller places. In fact, there is now an entire group referred to as *multiflorals* or *sweetheart* types that have many flowers up to 2 inches (3 cm) across on very compact growing plants. I've grown several of these and find them to be pure pleasure.

If space is at a premium, look for these specific plants or see if these miniatures have been used as parents in the plants that you're considering:

✔ *Phalaenopsis equestris:* A dwarf species that is often used as one of the parents for breeding dwarf growth habits.

✔ *Phalaenopsis* **Sogo Twinkle (see Figure 10-10):** Sogo is the name of a well-known orchid nursery in Taiwan that produces some excellent phalaenopsis including many that are small growers.

✔ *Doritaenopsis* **Purple Gem:** This dwarf variety most commonly comes in shades of pink and purple, but there are also white forms. It frequently blooms more than once a year.

✔ *Phalaenopsis* **Carmela's Pixie:** Produced by Carmella Orchids, a nursery in Hawaii that has long been a grower and breeder of fine moth orchids including this diminutive one.

✔ *Phalaenopsis* **Cassandra:** Displays a 2½-inch (6-cm) clear white flower with a yellow flush and light-brown barring on the lower, outermost parts of the flower and throat. Some forms are fragrant.

✔ *Phalaenopsis* **Be Tris:** This mini has been around quite a while. It's still offered and is commonly used as a parent to pass its small plant size on to its offspring.

✔ *Phalaenopsis* **Mini Mark 'Holm' (see Figure 10-11):** This plant is so charming. It has light floral-scented white flowers that are speckled in orange with an orange-red lip and that are a little over 1 inch (2.5 cm) across.

**Figure 10-10:** *Phalaenopsis* Sogo Twinkle is a compact gem that produces many charming flowers on a very small plant with short flower spikes.

Photograph courtesy of Marc Herzog

**Figure 10-11:** *Phalaenopsis* Mini Mark 'Holm' is a delightful miniature phalaenopsis that everyone has space for.

## Answering the call of the wild

Earlier in this chapter, I mentioned a number of phalaenopsis species that are fragrant. Here are some others that are not as commonly grown because many people prefer the newer varieties with larger, rounder flowers, but interest in species is increasing as people are starting to better appreciate their simple, less complicated look.

TIP

Here are some species that are worth considering:

- *Phalaenopsis amabilis:* This native of Indonesia is the parent of most of today's white hybrids. The white flower with a yellow lip can last for months. It is not as round as the newer hybrids, but it has its own grace.

- *Phalaenopsis buissoniania:* Unlike most of the other phalaenopsis species, this one bears its medium pink flowers on an upright, up to 3-foot (1-m) tall stem, rather than an arched flower stem.

- *Phalaenopsis cornu-cervi:* The flower stem on this species is flat and produces yellow, glossy flowers that are barred in maroon. Its flowers are borne sequentially, so don't cut off the flower spike, because new flowers will continue to arise from it.

© Steven A. Frowine

*Angranthes*
Grandalena
*(Angraecum magdalenae*
x *Aeranthes grandiflora)*

*Ascocenda*
Peggy Foo '#1'
*(Vanda* Bonnie Blue
'Fukumura'
x *Ascocentrum*
*curvifolium)*

© Steven A. Frowine

*Brassolaeliocattleya*
Formosa Gold

*Brassolaeliocattleya*
Harlequin 'Act II'
AM/AOS

*Brassocattleya*
Cynthia 'Pink Lady'
HCC/AOS

*Encyclia cordigera*

*Odontioda* Margarete Holm 'Alpine'
*(Odontoglossum* Bic-ross x *Odontioda* Adolf Rohl)

*Odontocidium*
Tiger Crow
'Golden Girl'
HCC/AOS

© STEVEN A. FROWINE

*Miltassia*
*(Brassia* Rex 'Pieper'
x *Miltonia* Honolulu
'Warne's Best')

© STEVEN A. FROWINE

*Vuylstekeara*
Yokara
'Perfection'
AM/AOS

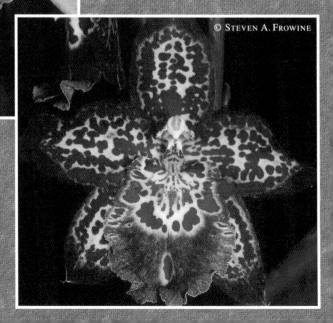

© STEVEN A. FROWINE

*Miltoniopsis*
Hajime Ono
*(Miltoniopsis*
Martin Orenstein x
*Miltoniopsis* Peach Ono*)*

*Dendrobium sulawesiense*

*Phalaenopsis*
Ambo
Buddha 'SW'

*Phalaenopsis*
New Cinderella x
*Doritaenopsis*
Taisuco 'Firebird'

*Phalaenopsis*
(*Phalaenopsis*
Gelblieber-violacea x
*Phalaenopsis* Coral Isles)

*Cochleanthes*
Amazing
*(Cochleanthes*
*flabelliformis* x
*Cochleanthes*
*amazonica)*

© STEVEN A. FROWINE

*Paphiopedilum* Maudiae

© STEVEN A. FROWINE

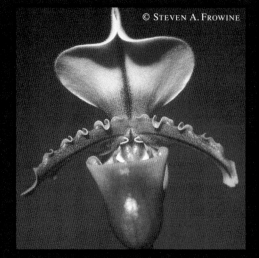

© Steven A. Frowine

© Steven A. Frowine

*Paphiopedilum*
Langley Pride
'Burlingame'
HCC/AOS

*Paphiopedilum*
*spicerianum*

*Paphiopedilum*
*sukhakulii*

© Steven A. Frowine

✔ *Phalaenopsis mariae:* The flower of this orchid is marked with bright spots of brown and red (see Figure 10-12). It will frequently have multiple, short flower spikes in the spring and summer.

✔ *Phalaenopsis schilleriana:* A parent of many of the pink hybrids sold today. Like *Phalaenopsis stuartiana,* a mature plant produces a flurry of flowers and its leaves are beautifully marbled.

✔ *Phalaenopsis stuartiana* (see **Figure 10-13**): A mature plant of this variety can have up to 100 white flowers on a branched spike. The foliage (refer to Figure 10-1) is beautifully patterned.

**Figure 10-12:** *Phalaenopsis mariae* sports a colorful pattern of brown and red spots on its glossy white flower.

Don't buy wild-collected plants. They deplete the natural population of these plants from their natives lands from which they have sometimes been illegally removed. Wild-collected plants take quite a while to become established, and their leaves are tattered from their jungle experience. Species phalaenopsis that have been nursery-grown from seed are generally more vigorous and will adjust better to a home environment. So, only buy from a grower or supplier who assures you that his orchids are seed-grown, not wild-collected.

**Figure 10-13:** *Phalaenopsis stuartiana* makes quite a show with its flurry of white flowers backed with stunning foliage.

# Oh, Give Me a Home . . . : Cultural Requirements

Moth orchids do well in medium to low light, similar to other houseplants like African violets. They also thrive in moderate humidity of 50 percent or so and average daytime temperatures of 70°F to 80°F (21°C to 26°C) during the day and about 65°F (18°C) at night.

Moth orchids are particularly susceptible to a disease commonly called *crown rot,* which is usually the result of water pooling in the small pocket formed at the new, young growth of the orchid. To prevent this disease, make sure this growing point stays dry overnight. If you need to, use a cotton swab to remove this extra moisture.

# Relatives of Moth Orchids

Moth orchids have various relatives that are also easy growers and good choices for beginners. These orchids have similar cultural requirements to moth orchids, unless otherwise noted, and come in different flower shapes and colors and many are fragrant.

---

## A moth with a 12-inch tongue!

*Angraecum sequipedale* was made famous by Charles Darwin who postulated that there must be a night-flying moth with a 12-inch tongue to be able to harvest the nectar from the flower of this orchid and in the process pollinate it. Darwin's scientific colleagues thought this belief to be preposterous. Thirty-five years after his death, he was proven right when a hawk moth, the pollinator for this orchid, with a 12-inch (30-cm) tongue, was found!

---

# *Africa's gift to orchid lovers: The Angraecoids*

Africa and its neighboring islands have always harbored mystery and intrigue with their fantastic fauna and flora. The orchids of this part of the world hold this same allure. Many of these orchids have waxy-white, star-shaped, heavenly scented flowers on plants with dark-green leathery leaves. Some are humongous and would only fit in a greenhouse with plenty of room, while others are of a manageable size or even miniature. In general, they require more light than phalaenopsis but have the same preference for warm, humid growing areas.

All angraecoids can be a bit touchy about repotting, so grow them in a fresh, long-lasting mix or mount them, so you don't have to repot them often.

### *A few of the big fellows*

If you have plenty of space, here are a few spectacular orchids that are worth your consideration:

✔ *Angraecum sequipedale:* Commonly called the Star of Bethlehem or the King of Angraecums, this Madagascan native is a spectacular orchid with 4½-inch (11-cm) waxy white blossoms blessed with the heady fragrance of jasmine (see Figure 10-14). Because this plant prefers very strong light and ultimately grows up to 3 feet (1 meter) tall and wide, it requires a large sunroom or a greenhouse.

✔ *Angraecum* **Longiscott:** Quite a showy angraecum hybrid, the plant grows 36 inches (90 cm) high and 12 inches (30 cm) wide. It produces 3-inch (7.5-cm) waxy, white lipped flowers with greenish sepals with 8- to 10-inch (20- to 25-cm) spurs that are borne on up to 24-inch (60-cm) arching spikes. It has a jasmine scent and is a reliable bloomer.

**Figure 10-14:** *Angraecum sequipedale* has a waxy, fragrant flower that can last for months.

## These might be more your size

Not everyone has the growing room necessary to accommodate the burly plants described earlier, so these smaller cousins may be a better choice for most. They have the same waxy, white, long-lasting flowers with delightful fragrances, but on much smaller plants.

✔ *Angraecum compactum:* As the second Latin name suggests, this is a more manageable sized plant that is about 10 inches (25 cm) wide and 12 to 14 inches (30 to 35 cm) high. It is a slow grower, but easy to grow, and it dependably produces 3-inch (7.5 cm), waxy-white, citrus-scented flowers after it's established.

✔ *Angraecum leonis:* This species is very popular because of its handsome green compact habit, about 6 to 10 inches (15 to 25 cm) high and wide with a relatively large 1½-inch (4-cm) waxy white flower (see Figure 10-15).

### Some smaller Angraecum relatives

Here are some charmers that are nice additions to your collection, all very fragrant:

✔ *Aerangis citrata:* This is an easy choice, an adaptable plant that thrives in lower light conditions and is a very compact grower. It blooms several times a year and has a light lemon fragrance (see Figure 10-16).

🗸 *Aerangis fastuosa:* Another gem with compact glossy green foliage with up to six flowers, with the fragrance of tuberose, in bloom at once.

🗸 *Angranthes* **Grandalena:** This is one of my favorites because as this plant matures, it produces multiple growths with recurring, almost constant blooming. It produces 3-inch (7.5-cm), green-white spurred, jasmine-scented flowers borne singly that show off against its very compact, glossy, dark-green leaves.

**Figure 10-15:** *Angraecum leonis* is a smaller grower that will fit anyone's growing space.

**Figure 10-16:** *Aerangis citrata* displays up to 30 flowers in arching sprays.

## *Vandas and some of their close cousins*

Anyone who has been to Hawaii is familiar with the orchids that are used in the welcoming leis; most often, they're vandas. Sadly, the varieties used for these flowery necklaces are ones only suitable for growing in Hawaii and other very bright areas. Fortunately, there are others in this group that are less demanding but still can be quite a challenge for many home growers because of their higher light requirements. If you live in warmer, higher light areas of the country, like Hawaii, Florida, or parts of California, these plants are more doable.

Large strap-leaved vandas are simply gorgeous and are found in a wide range of colors including heavenly blues (see Figure 10-17), cotton-candy pinks, sunny yellows, and hot oranges. The flowers can be quite huge, 5 to 6 inches (12.5 to 15 cm) across on some hybrids.

Although they don't require as bright light as some of the other vandas, they still present quite a challenge to home growers in the northern part of the United States who experience heavy cloud cover and short, dark days in the winter. To grow them in these areas, you need to have an exceptionally sunny southern window or a hobby greenhouse. I've grown and bloomed some of them under high-intensity lights, but you don't want to know what my electric bill was!

**Figure 10-17:** This strap-leaved variety, *Vanda* Kasem's Delight, shows the typical large round flowers of today's superb quality varieties.

Ascocendas are the result of breeding the larger vandas with a much smaller growing group of plants called ascocentrums. Their flowers may not be quite as giant as the 6-inch (15 cm) flowered strap-leaved vandas, but they can still be showstoppers and their smaller stature makes them much easier to manage. Grow them in a sunny window or close to florescent lights. Search out those that have the smaller sized growth habit.

Ascocendas come in a wide range of colors with many different varieties. Here are a few of the classics:

✔ *Ascocenda* **Yip Sum Wah:** The most famous of all ascocendas. It is most commonly found in bright oranges or reds, sometimes in purples, but it's also available in shades of yellow. It's noted for its prolific blooming and relatively compact habit.

✔ *Ascocenda* **Peggy Foo:** Another fine performer with clear, glossy red flowers on a compact plant (see the color insert for a full-color photo).

✔ *Ascocenda* **Medasand:** Still used in breeding to produce superior plants. Plants like *Ascocenda* Medasand are frequently grown in teak baskets like the one shown in Figure 10-18, because they afford the excellent drainage that ascocendas and vandas love. They can also be grown in pots as long as there are plenty of holes in the bottom of the containers.

**Figure 10-18:** *Ascocenda* Medasand in a teak basket.

Here is an assortment of different vanda-type orchids that I recommend:

- *Aerides odorata:* Bears clove-scented white flowers with purple spots on a pendulous flower spike. Leaves are about 10 inches (25 cm) long, but the stem grows quite tall, so this plant would be suitable in a bright window, but not under lights.

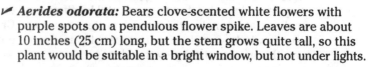

- *Neofinetia falcata:* This dwarf plant, 3 to 6 inches (7.5 to 10 cm) high with waxy white flowers about 1 inch (2.5cm) wide is easy to bloom on a bright windowsill or under lights. It's frequently used as a parent to impart its compact growth habit and vanilla fragrance to its offspring (see Figure 10-19). Commonly called the Japanese Wind Orchid, this was once the exclusive property of the Royal Family of Japan. Commoners were forbidden to have it in their possession. Its cultivation dates many centuries back to the Edo period in Japan. It was first described in 1784.

- *Neostylis* **Lou Sneary:** This has been a very successful variety that has a compact habit (inherited from one of its parents, *Neofinetia falcata*). It comes in various color forms — white, pink, and blue. All produce a flurry of 1-inch (2.5-cm) fragrant flowers and make super plants for growing on the windowsill or under lights.

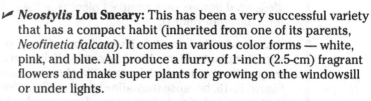

- *Ascofinetia* **Cherry Blossom:** Another compact beauty with lightly fragrant rose-lavender flowers that is the result of breeding an ascocentrum with our Japanese friend, neofinetia.

- *Renanthera monachica:* Many of the renantheras are huge plants that can get several feet tall and so are a bit of a challenge to handle in the house. This is a dazzling dwarf form that takes years to get up to 1 foot (30 cm). Its flowers are the colors of a bright yellow-orange flame (see Figure 10-20).

- *Rhynchostylis gigantea:* When you smell the intoxicating citrus fragrance of this orchid, commonly called foxtail orchid because of the shape of its pendulous cluster of flowers, you will be hooked. This can eventually become a quite large orchid, but it will take many years to get there. This one performs great in a sunny window. There are several color forms including the most common white with purple spots, all white, and solid burgundy red, at times referred to as the Sagarik Strain (see Figure 10-21).

- *Rhynchostylis retusa:* This looks very similar to the preceding plant and its flower color range is similar. The flowers tend to be smaller but there are usually more of them on longer flower spikes.

- *Rhynchostylis coelestis:* Unlike the other two rhynchostylis, this one has upright flower spikes and the most common form has blue and white flowers. Other color forms are pink and white.

✔ **Sedirea japonica:** Another gift from Asia that not many Western orchidists are familiar with. After I witnessed this orchid being judged for its lemon fragrance at the New York International Orchid Show, I made a beeline for the vendor who was selling this charmer. I found myself behind a long line of mostly Asian folks ahead of me who fully appreciated this orchid's merits. It's like a dwarf phalaenopsis in its growth habit, with about 6-inch (15-cm) leaves and has the same cultural requirements.

**Figure 10-19:** *Neofinetia falcata* — commonly called the Japanese Wind Orchid.

**Figure 10-20:** *Renanthera monachica* is a delightful, small, and brightly colored orchid.

**Figure 10-21:** The foxtail orchid, *Rhynchostylis gigantea,* fills up an entire room with its citrus fragrance, and its pendulous flower spike in full bloom is a splendid sight.

# Chapter 11

# The Quintessential Orchids: Cattleyas and Their Relatives

● ● ● ● ● ● ● ● ● ● ● ● ● ● ● ● ● ● ● ● ● ● ● ● ● ● ● ● ● ● ● ● ● ● ● ● ● ● ● ● ● ● ● ●

*In This Chapter*

▶ Understanding how cattleyas and laelias made it from nature to your home

▶ Growing cattleyas' wild relatives

▶ Looking at the man-made cattleya orchids

▶ Discovering small-growing cattleyas, the minicatts

● ● ● ● ● ● ● ● ● ● ● ● ● ● ● ● ● ● ● ● ● ● ● ● ● ● ● ● ● ● ● ● ● ● ● ● ● ● ● ● ● ● ● ●

*W*hen people picture what a typical orchid looks like, the cattleya flower is usually what comes to mind. Years ago, the ultimate gift to give your mother or grandmother on Mother's Day was a cattleya orchid corsage. Back then, these were usually fragrant flowers in various shades of lavender.

Until the skyrocketing popularity of the phalaenopsis took off several years ago, the cattleyas were the undisputed kings of orchids. They're still highly popular, because they offer huge and frequently fragrant flowers, in a complete spectrum of colors and flower shapes, on plants varying in size from a few inches (5 cm) to a few feet (60 cm) tall. To see how the glorious flowers of cattleyas are constructed, see Figure 11-1.

In this chapter, I introduce you to a few of the many orchids in this illustrious group that are readily available and easy to grow. You'll see why they epitomize the beauty and fragrance that only orchids can offer.

Cattleyas grow best in moderate humidity and medium to bright light, with good air circulation, and in intermediate temperatures. For general cultural information, see Chapter 7.

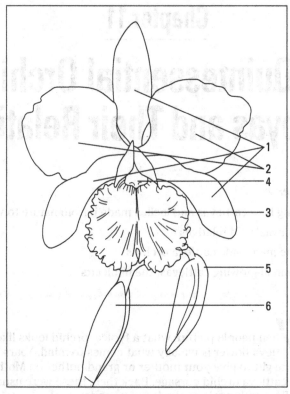

**Figure 11-1:** The structure of a typical cattleya flower
(1 = Sepals; 2 = Petals; 3 = Lip; 4 = Column; 5 = Bud; 6 = Sheath).

# From the Jungles to Your Home

In the 1800s, plant collectors and explorers risked their lives and lived in steamy tropical outposts to bring these South American orchids to the plant lovers of Europe. Today, all the best forms are readily available and none have been collected from the wild. Instead, the best cattleyas are raised from seed in laboratory flasks, which is not only good news from a conservation stand-point (they aren't resulting in destroyed natural habitats from field collecting) but also because these plants are generally stronger and more vigorous than those collected from the wild and adapt better to home-growing situations.

# *Some selected cattleya species*

Some of the cattleya species are a little more of a challenge to grow than the hybrids, so if you want to go right to the easier plants, skip this section and move on to "The Queens of the Ball: Cattleya Hybrids," later in this chapter.

However, if you prefer the simple, classic flower that the species offers, here are some to try that are usually readily available:

- ✔ *Cattleya amethystoglossa:* You'll need a tall, very bright window to accommodate this orchid, because it can reach 3 feet (1 meter) in height. Its 2½-inch (7-cm) light pink flowers speckled with purple and highlighted with a purple lip are in clusters of up to a dozen and appear in the spring.

- ✔ *Cattleya aurantiaca:* A longtime favorite with dark green shiny leaves on a compact 12-inch (30-cm) plant, this orchid is loaded with clusters of orange to red, 1½ to 2-inch (4- to 5-cm) flowers.

- ✔ *Cattleya bicolor:* Clusters of 3-inch (7.5-cm) coppery to pinkish-brown, waxy, spicy-scented flowers with contrasting bright-pink lips that appear in the spring make this species a standout. The plant grows to about 20 to 36 inches (50 to 85 cm) tall. Repot this orchid only when new roots are starting to develop.

- ✔ *Cattleya guttata:* This orchid is very similar in most respects to *Cattleya amethystoglossa,* except that it blooms in the summer and fall.

- ✔ *Cattleya harrisoniana* (see **Figure 11-2**): Pink to deep rose, floral-scented flowers are displayed on this summer or fall bloomer. This plant is best repotted in the spring.

- ✔ *Cattleya intermedia:* A medium-size grower that reaches about 15 inches (40 cm) high with leaves about 6 inches (15 cm) long, this orchid produces sizable, 6-inch (15-cm) sweet floral-scented flowers that are a light pink with a contrasting dark purple lip.

- ✔ *Cattleya leuddemanniana:* Up to five 4½ to 5-inch (10- to 13-cm) richly purple flowers veined in yellow adorn this floral-scented, spring-blooming plant.

- ✔ *Cattleya maxima* (see **Figure 11-3**): Loaded with 5-inch (12.5-cm) lavender-pink, baby-powder-scented flowers that display lips with dark purple veins and yellow throats, this fall- to early-winter-blooming orchid is Peru's national flower.

**Figure 11-2:** *Cattleya harrisoniana* has been a longtime favorite cattleya species.

Some tall-growing cattleyas can be very top-heavy, especially when they're in full bloom. Potting them in squat, azalea-type clay pots that have wider bases and/or putting 1 inch (2.5 cm) or so of clean gravel in the bottom of the pots helps prevent the plants from toppling over.

**Figure 11-3:** Peru is proud to have the *Cattleya maxima* as its national flower.

## The real truth about flower color

Orchid flower color descriptions in catalogs sometimes reflect more what the breeder or seller of orchids would *prefer* the flower color to be than what it actually *is*. When the flower color is described as "yellow," "pink," "white," or "orange," it's usually close to this. When the color descriptions drift toward solid blues and clear reds, this is where wishful thinking sometimes takes over. Most "blues" are actually bluish shades of purple or lavender, and most "reds" are actually dark-oranges.

## *Some selected laelia species*

Laelias look very much like cattleyas. In fact, few amateurs are able to tell them apart. One difference: Laelias usually have somewhat of a smaller lip than cattleyas. Laelias are native to the same areas as their close cousins, cattleyas, and have very similar cultural requirements.

Following is a sampling of some of the easier and more beautiful laelias that are worthy of space in your orchid collection:

- ✔ *Laelia anceps* (see Figure 11-4): This orchid is a toughie that's hardy to 20°F (–6.6°C) and is a favorite for growing outdoors in mild parts of California and the southeastern United States. It comes in various color forms but most commonly has clusters of two to six 2½ to 3-inch (6- to 8-cm) light lavender flowers with darker purple lips and throats. The flower spike can reach up to 3 feet (1 meter), so be sure to give it plenty of headroom when it sends up its flower spikes.

- ✔ *Laelia perrinii:* A native of Brazil, this species is not yet commonly found, but it's sure to increase in popularity because it's a robust grower, reaching about 14 to 16 inches (30 to 40 cm) in height. It sports lightly spice-scented, fine-quality, lavender flowers measuring up to 6 inches (15 cm) across, with lips that are trumpet-shaped and edged with deep violet with white in the throat. Blue and white color forms are also available.

- ✔ *Laelia pumila:* A compact grower that only reaches a height of 8 inches (20 cm), this species is frequently grown mounted on a slab of tree fern or cork. It has a short flower spike with one to two lightly floral-scented flowers that average 3 to 4 inches (8 to 10 cm) across. The entire flower is lavender-colored, sometimes with a darker lip. It comes in other color forms, including a blue one.

✔ *Laelia purpurata:* This orchid is frequently referred to as the "Queen of Laelias," because it has the largest and showiest flowers of its genus. This is a glorious plant with flowers that vary quite a bit from plant to plant but generally are about 6 inches (15 cm) across, white, frequently with violet-blue lips (there are various lip colors), and a spicy or anise scent. It needs to be grown on the cooler and drier side during the winter months to bloom best in the spring to summer.

**Figure 11-4:** *Laelia anceps* bears its flowers on tall, elegant spikes.

## Other cattleya relatives

A slew of other orchid species are closely related to cattleyas and laelias. In the following sections, I tip you off to some good performers from this group.

### Brassavolas

You'll find several excellent brassavola species, but the one that leads the pack because of its popularity and ease of growing (with the same cultural requirements as cattleyas) is *Brassavola nodosa* (shown in Figure 11-5), commonly called "Lady of the Night," because of its enchanting and permeating evening fragrance. One to six of its spidery greenish white flowers, from 3 to 6 inches (7.5 to 15 cm) across, are borne on a 6-inch (15-cm) flower stem. It's a clump-forming orchid that gives its best show when it *isn't* divided.

**Figure 11-5:** *Brassavola nodosa* is often recommended as a beginner's orchid because of its ease of culture.

Other brassavolas worth considering are

- ✔ *Brassavola cordata:* Has up to 20 lime green, 2-inch (5-cm) blooms with heart-shaped lips. Usually blooms twice a year.

- ✔ *Brassavola cucullata:* Has spidery, exotic white to green flowers that are sometimes tinged with yellow or burgundy. Blooms in the summer to fall.

- ✔ *Brassavola flagellaris:* Relatively unknown but easy to grow. Its flower is similar in shape and color to the others in this group, but it's blessed with a wonderful hot-chocolate fragrance.

- ✔ *Brassavola martiana:* Its flower is white with a fringed lip and green-yellow points.

- ✔ *Brassavola perrinii:* This species has one of the largest flowers of the brassavolas. It usually blooms in the summer but can be variable.

### Broughtonia

*Broughtonia sanguinea* (shown in Figure 11-6) is a small grower, 3 to 4 inches (8 to 10 cm) high, with clusters of 1-inch (2.5-cm) reddish-purple, pink, magenta to crimson flowers, usually veined in dark purple on an 8- to 16-inch (20- to 40-cm) stem. This orchid blooms in the summer and likes a very bright spot. Water and fertilize it regularly during its peak growth in the summertime.

**Figure 11-6:** *Broughtonia sanguinea* is a charmer native to Cuba and Jamaica.

## Encyclias

This group contains some of the easiest of all orchids to grow and bloom. Many of them are also fragrant.

- ✔ *Encyclia adenocaula:* Most encyclias are shades of green and white with some purple markings. This Mexican beauty is different, with rosy-pink to magenta, star-shaped flowers that are borne on long branched sprays.

- ✔ *Encyclia cochleata* **(see Figure 11-7):** Commonly called the "cockleshell" or "clamshell" orchid because its upside-down flower lip looks like one, this unique-looking orchid is very easy to grow and often blooms several times a year. The lip is streaked with purple, while the rest of the spidery shaped flower is lime green.

- ✔ *Encyclia cordigera:* Not only is this species considered to be one of the handsomest in the encyclia group, it also fills the air with the fragrance of vanilla. It displays clusters of deep maroon flowers with bright pink lips. The plant is modest in size and grows 12 to 15 inches (30 to 37 cm) tall. See the color photographs in the center of this book for an example.

- ✔ *Encyclia fragrans:* The flower of this very-easy-to-grow orchid is a 2-inch (5-cm) subtle green with purple stripes in the lip. This orchid is so well-liked because it's so easy to grow and bloom and because it emits a heavy gardenia fragrance.

- ✔ *Encyclia radiata* **(see Figure 11-8):** The subtle creamy white, cockleshell-type flowers with purple stripes in the lip, borne in clusters, are not what make this orchid so popular — though they *could* be. Instead, its ease of growing and blooming and wonderful fragrance — which has been variously described as smelling spicy-floral or like coconut cream pie, lilac, cinnamon, and hyacinth — are what keep people coming back to this orchid.

✔ *Encyclia tampense:* A Florida native that is hardy as far north as the central part of the state, this encyclia has green flowers overlaid with brown with white lips marked with purple blotches. It emits a sweet scent when it flowers in the summer.

**Figure 11-7:** *Encyclia cochleata* is recommended as an ideal beginner's orchid because it's so easy to grow and blooms on an almost constant basis.

**Figure 11-8:** The claim to fame of the *Encyclia radiata* is its sweet-scented flowers.

### Epidendrum

This group is filled with very brightly colored members and some have a very strong resemblance to encyclias.

- *Epidendrum ciliare* **(see Figure 11-9):** The 3- to 6-inch (7.5- to 15-cm) lime-green petals of this orchid are set off by its exquisite white fringed lip. The plant reaches about 16 inches (40 cm) tall and is said to have the fragrance of grapefruit.

- *Epidendrum difforme:* This orchid has glossy green flowers about 1¼ inches (3 cm) on short spikes with a medicinal scent.

- *Epidendrum cinnabarinum:* Bright-orange 1½-inch (4-cm) flowers with fringed yellow lips are the main feature of this colorful epidendrum. The flowers are borne in succession, so the plant can be in bloom for months during the summer. This orchid can grow quite tall, up to 4 feet (120 cm), and is often grown in large, mass plantings in semitropical to tropical climates.

- *Epidendrum stamfordianum:* A large, well-grown plant of this type of orchid is something to see. It's loaded with spikes of hundreds of fragrant, 2-inch (5-cm) yellow flowers painted in burgundy with white and yellow lips. It usually blooms in late winter to early spring.

**Figure 11-9:** *Epidendrum ciliare* has a spidery green flower with a delicate white fringed lip.

### Sophronitis

The sophronitis genus primarily consists of dwarf-growing plants with oversized red and orange cattleya-shaped flowers that shimmer in the sunlight. If you see any of them at a greenhouse for sale — for example, *Sophronitis grandiflora* (orange-red, shown in Figure 11-10), *Sophronitis coccinea* (scarlet), or *Sophronitis cernua* (orange) — you'll surely want to buy one.

**Figure 11-10:** *Sophronitis grandiflora* is a charming plant, but it can be quite a challenge to grow and bloom. A better choice may be a hybrid that uses one of the sophronitis species as a parent.

But don't! At least not until you have several years of orchid growing under your belt. These diminutive darlings can be very tricky to grow and bloom. You're much better off purchasing a hybrid that has used one of these species as a parent (see "Hot reds and oranges" and "Minicatts," later in this chapter). These hybrids are more vigorous, easier to flower, and much less demanding.

# The Queens of the Ball: Cattleya Hybrids

A modern, standard-size cattleya hybrid in full bloom is a sight to behold! Thanks to the skill of orchid hybridizers and the breeding willingness of cattleyas and their relatives to participate in this process, the results have been flowers in a breathtaking array of colors and heady fragrances.

Because cattleya breeding has progressed to such a high state of perfection, it's actually difficult to pick out a bad one. In the following sections, I show you a few of the many outstanding hybrids, arranged by approximate color group.

## Pristine whites

White cattleyas are almost as classic as the lavender ones. The modern hybrids have full, round, and fragrant flowers. Here are two old classics that are still popular:

- ✔ *Brassocattleya* **Mount Hood:** This orchid is a pristine white with a golden-yellow lip and the heady fragrance of vanilla.

- ✔ *Cattleya* **Bow Bells:** This is another old-timer that you'll find in the background of many of today's hybrids. It has fine form and its frilly lip is marked on the inside with a touch of yellow.

## Purples, pinks, lavenders, and blues

Purple hybrids have been around a long time. You can't go wrong in buying any in this color group — they're all very good to excellent. The blue shades in cattleyas are newer. Most of the purples are fragrant. Here are just a few possibilities:

- ✔ *Brassocattleya* **Blue Grotto:** This orchid is referred to as a blue, but it's more like a violet purple.

- ✔ *Brassocattleya* **Norman's Bay 'Low's' FCC/AOS:** Although first introduced in England in 1946, this is still a standard bearer today of purple cattleya breeding and is still used as a parent.

- ✔ *Brassocattleya* **Pamela Hetherington 'Coronation' FCC/AOS:** Named for a family member of the illustrious cattleya breeder, Ernest Hetherington, this is a 6-inch (15-cm) lavender-pink flower with a pink ruffled lip and orange-yellow throat. Its flower is a superb shape and is strongly fragrant.

- ✔ *Cattleya* **Irene Holguin:** This is a lavender orchid with excellent shape and color.

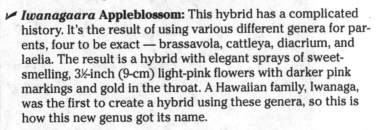

- *Laeliocattleya* **Bonanza Queen:** A classic 6-inch (15-cm) lavender with gold veins in the throat.

- *Iwanagaara* **Appleblossom:** This hybrid has a complicated history. It's the result of using various different genera for parents, four to be exact — brassavola, cattleya, diacrium, and laelia. The result is a hybrid with elegant sprays of sweet-smelling, 3½-inch (9-cm) light-pink flowers with darker pink markings and gold in the throat. A Hawaiian family, Iwanaga, was the first to create a hybrid using these genera, so this is how this new genus got its name.

## Hot reds and oranges

Most of the red hybrids are compact growers because a frequent parent in these is one of the sophronitis, which are both red and very dwarf. Here are some to look for — either as plants you'll grow, or in the parentage of the plants you're considering:

- *Sophrolaeliocattleya* **Jewel Box 'Scheherazade' AM/AOS (see Figure 11-11):** An older hybrid that is still popular today because of its manageable size, clear red flowers, and easy culture.

- *Sophrolaeliocattleya* **Jewel Box 'Dark Waters':** Another popular one that is a very dark red clone.

- *Brassolaeliocattleya* **Oconee:** A large-flowered orchid, with fragrant, red-purple flowers with a dark red lip.

- *Brassolaeliocattleya* **Edisto:** Large purple-red, with up to five flowers per stem. This is a fall bloomer.

- *Brassolaeliocattleya* **Owen Holmes 'Mendenhall' AM/AOS:** Considered one of the best of all reds, it's frequently used as a parent to pass its superior coloring to its offspring. A good choice.

- *Sophrolaeliocattleya* **Hazel Boyd:** Another winner with various bright-orange tones and excellent plant vigor.

- *Cattleya* **Chocolate Drop 'Kodama' AM/AOS:** This one has clusters of glossy burgundy flowers with yellow on the column and the fragrance of lily-of-the-valley.

Figure 11-11: *Sophrolaeliocattleya* Jewel Box 'Scheherazade' AM/AOS still remains a favorite.

## Sunny yellows

Fine yellows have been a more recent development. Today's hybrids range from gold to butter yellow. Some are sold yellow, while others have darker colored red or purple splotched lips. A few names you can look for include the following:

- ✔ *Brassocattleya* **Goldenzelle 'Lemon Chiffon' (see Figure 11-12):** A fine example of how far yellow flowers in cattleya hybrids have come, this one sports 6-inch (15-cm) lemon-yellow flowers with a splash of deep red on the lip. This is a winter bloomer.

- ✔ *Brassocattleya* **Formosan Gold:** Its dark-red ruffled lip provides a dramatic contrast with its golden-yellow petals and sepals that have a spread of about 4½ inches (11 cm) across. See the color photographs in the center of the book for a look at this orchid.

- ✔ *Brassocattleya* **Malworth 'Orchidglade' FCC/AOS:** Highly awarded and one of the best known yellows.

- ✔ *Laeliocattleya* **Lorraine Shirae:** A bright yellow with a contrasting red lip.

- ✔ *Potinara* **Twentyfour Carat:** A large, handsome, clear gold-yellow.

- ✔ *Potinara* **Haw Yuan Gold:** The Taiwan orchid breeders have been making notable contributions to the cattleya group, and this award-winner with its 6-inch (15-cm) bicolor bloom — yellow petals and darker yellow lip — is one of them.

**Figure 11-12:** *Brassocattleya* Goldenzelle 'Lemon Chiffon' AM/AOS is a gorgeous soft lemon-yellow that demonstrates well the advances in breeding. This one is a frequent winner at orchid shows.

## Cool greens

There is something refreshing about lime-green flowers. They have their own following of orchid lovers. Some of their flowers have very fringed lips, usually inherited from the species *Rhyncholaelia digbyana* (formerly know as *Brassavola digbyana*). This unique species is also noted for its strong fragrance. Some of the greens have clear-colored flowers, while others are blotched in purple. Here are some choices to consider:

✔ *Brassocattleya* **Greenwich:** This cross was made in the late 1960s but still shows up in today's offerings. The flower is about 4 inches across with purple markings on its fringed lip.

✔ *Brassocattleya* **Ports of Paradise 'Emerald Isle' HCC/AOS:** One of the most awarded of the greens, this orchid offers large lime-green flowers, a strong fragrance, and a ruffled lip.

✔ *Brassocattleya* **Rio's Green Magic (see Figure 11-13):** This hybrid shows, with its deeply fringed lip, the influence of the species *Rhyncholaelia digbyana*. It has large, 5-inch (13-cm) flowers.

**Figure 11-13:** *Brassocattleya* Rio's Green Magic offers unique beauty and a sensuous fragrance.

## Bring out the clowns: Splash petals and flares

This group is commonly called "clowns" because of the sense of gaiety their wild color combinations impart. They're marked with two or more splashes or flares of contrasting colors, and the results can be quite dramatic.

- ✔ **Cattleya intermedia var. aquinii:** This is the orchid that really started it all. It was the first one that displayed flares of color in the petals and lip, so it was used extensively in hybridizing to pass this quality on to its offspring. In this case, the coloring was purple flares on white petals and the lip. This variety is sometimes offered for sale these days but is more frequently found in the parentage of many of the newer splash petals and flares.

- ✔ **Brassocattleya Momilani Rainbow:** A real showstopper with 6-inch (15-cm) flowers and light lavender-pink sepals, dark pink petals, and lips with bright splashes of lemon yellow on them.

- ✔ **Laeliocattleya Colorama 'The Clown':** Another old classic that has proven invaluable as a parent for future splash-petaled varieties, this orchid has white petals and purple flares with a larger flower than *Cattleya intermedia* var. *aquinii*.

- ✔ **Laeliocattleya Gaiety Flambeau:** A more modern hybrid that has large clusters of white flowers with purple flares.

✔ *Laeliocattleya* **Mari's Song 'CTM 217':** This is one of the best and most popular tricolored, splash-petaled varieties. It has a yellow and white flower with magenta flares and lip with pink sepals and a yellow throat. What a grand color combo! On top of that, it's very fragrant.

✔ *Potinara* **Barana Beauty 'Burana' HCC/AOS (see Figure 11-14):** A compact grower that reaches about 12 inches (30 cm) tall, its 3½-inch (9-cm) citrus-scented flowers are a yellow-green with red flares. Frequently blooms twice a year.

**Figure 11-14:** *Potinara* Barana Beauty 'Burana' HCC/AOS offers clusters of citrus-scented green flowers with red flares.

## Fashionable art shades

This is a catchall category that includes cattleya-type hybrids that combine a range of pastel colors. Here are a few of the many nice ones:

✔ *Brassolaeliocattleya* **George King:** A salmon-peachy, fragrant, 6-inch (15-cm) flower with crystalline texture and the fact that this one often blooms more than once a year make this a popular selection.

✔ *Brassolaeliocattleya* **Harlequin 'Act II':** Another flower with a mixed palette of colors including peach, yellow, and purple flares. A sumptuous beauty. See the color photographs in the center of this book for an example.

✔ *Brassolaeliocattleya* **Hawaiian Avalanche (see Figure 11-15):** This orchid shows off a delightful display of tropical color with the 6-inch (15-cm) apricot-pink flowers with a golden-orange fringed lip and purple streak down the center of the lip.

**Figure 11-15:** *Brassolaeliocattleya* Hawaiian Avalanche provides a riot of color. In this close-up of the lip, you can get an idea of the play of color and patterns.

For standard cattleyas, purchasing clones is usually your best bet. (See Chapter 2 for more information on clones or meristems.) They're very reasonably priced, you'll know exactly what they'll look like, and their flowers will usually be superior to the standard hybrids.

# Minicatts

There is a revolution going on now in cattleya breeding! Small is in — at least in plant size. Although there is no denying that full-size cattleyas in bloom are impressive, unfortunately they also take up a lot of growing space. And for windowsill and under-light growers, where every square inch counts, this creates a problem. This is where minicatts (short for *miniature cattleyas*) come in.

They have no special cultural requirements that differ from the standard, full-size plants: Because they're commonly planted in small clay pots, they tend to dry up more quickly than the larger plants in bigger pots, so you need to keep a sharper eye on your watering to make sure they don't get too dry.

## The key players

These are the species with miniature to small growth habits that have been the principal contributors to this breeding effort. Each of these species is popular in its own right, but each has also been even more important for contributing its desirable characteristics to future orchid generations:

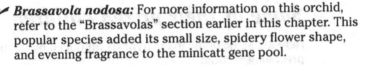

✔ ***Brassavola nodosa:*** For more information on this orchid, refer to the "Brassavolas" section earlier in this chapter. This popular species added its small size, spidery flower shape, and evening fragrance to the minicatt gene pool.

✔ ***Cattleya aclandiae:*** A little dazzler with 3- to 4-inch (7- to 13-cm) yellowish-green to brown flowers covered with purple spots and accentuated with a magenta lip, this is not an easy species to grow. Stick to its hybrids to get the visual effects of the species without its demanding cultural requirements.

✔ ***Cattleya luteola* (see Figure 11-16):** This is a darling plant that only reaches 5 to 7 inches (12 to 17.5 cm) tall, making it perfect for small spaces. Its fresh, floral-scented, 2-inch (5-cm), pale yellow flowers with a darker lip are borne in sprays of two to five in the spring.

✔ ***Cattleya walkeriana:*** This diminutive orchid has a lot going for it. It has a miniature stature, making it ideal for growing under lights or on a windowsill. Its rose-purple flowers of heavy substance have a fine shape and an exquisite vanilla and sweet floral fragrance that is strongest in the morning. It's also found in an *alba* (white) that tends to have the best flower form.

✔ ***Laelia briegeri:*** This is a miniature bright-yellow species that isn't easy to grow by itself but has been valuable for its color and dwarf growing habit that it imparts to its hybrids.

✔ ***Laelia pumila:*** This is another important contributor for it compact growth habit, flower form, and color.

✔ ***Sophronitis coccinea:*** The shimmering red color and miniature plant habit made this plant an important link. Refer to Figure 11-12 to see a species, *Sophronitis grandiflora,* that looks very much like this one.

**Figure 11-16:** *Cattleya luteola* is a cutie with a fresh floral scent that is strongest in the morning.

## Some of their prized children

Here are some of the many hybrids produced by the parents in the preceding section:

- ✔ *Brassocattleya* **Binosa (see Figure 11-17):** Combines a striking color combination, 3-inch (5-cm) bright-green flower with a white flared lip, dusted with purple speckles, with a sweet spicy evening perfume inherited from one of its parents, *Brassavola nodosa*.

- ✔ *Brassocattleya* **Cynthia:** An offspring of *Cattleya walkeriana*, this variety is very compact, has 4-inch (20-cm) full, round-pink fragrant flowers with yellow in the throat. It frequently blooms twice a year.

- ✔ *Cattleya* **Brabantiae:** One of the first hybrids to be made, in the 1800s, this one has *Cattleya aclandiae* as one of its parents. Its 2½-inch (6-cm), thick, waxy, pink, fragrant flowers are spotted with maroon and serve as a backdrop for a stunning white lip and column edged in purple. It only grows to 6 to 8 inches (15 to 20 cm) tall and is still popular today.

- ✔ *Cattleya* **Peckhaviensis (see Figure 11-18):** This orchid shows off purple spotted flowers with a bright-pink lip much like one of its parents, *Cattleya aclandiae*.

- ✔ *Laeliocattleya* **Angel Love (see Figure 11-19):** An easy-to-grow fragrant orchid that has perfectly formed, 4-inch (10-cm), lavender-pink flowers with a frilled lip and yellow in the throat.

- ✔ *Laeliocattleya* **Love Knot:** Another *Cattleya walkeriana* child that is a very small grower, with large 4-inch (10-cm), deep-red-purple flowers with a darker lip. This one is also fragrant and blooms twice a year.

- ✔ *Laeliocattleya* **Mini Purple:** An offspring of *Laelia pumila* and *Cattleya walkeriana*, this is one of the best known and available of the minicatts. It has lavender flowers with a darker purple lip and is fragrant.

- ✔ *Sophrocattleya* **Beaufort:** A classic that has as a parent *Cattleya luteola*, this orchid is found in various shades of orange and red. It continues to be used extensively as a parent to produce new miniature hybrids.

- ✔ *Sophrocattleya* **Crystelle Smith:** Frequently winning ribbons at shows because of its fine form and delicious color combinations that can vary from pastel pink to apricot shades with lips of solid yellow or marked with red.

✔ *Sophrolaelia* **Psyche:** Another old-timer, this is a miniature with petite flaming orange-red flowers passed on from its sophronitis parent. Fortunately, it's easy to grow.

✔ *Sophrolaeliocattleya* **Jewel Box:** See "Hot reds and oranges," earlier in this chapter.

✔ *Sophrolaeliocattleya* **Mahalo Jack:** I've enjoyed growing this orchid. It has a solid red flower on a dwarf plant. Most are fragrant and bloom a few times a year.

**Figure 11-17:** *Brassocattleya* Binosa 'Kirk' AMAOS combines a sweet scent with a striking color combination.

**Figure 11-18:** *Cattleya* Peckhaviensis show its spots and bright magenta lip from *Cattleya aclandiae*.

**Figure 11-19:** *Laeliocattleya* Angel Love is a perfectly shaped dwarf *Cattleya* with a citrus fragrance.

# Chapter 12

# Slipper Orchids

L ady's slippers are some of the easiest orchids to grow and among the most rewarding orchids you'll find, making them a great orchid for beginners. They present a wide range of strikingly colored, frequently glossy flowers in myriad shapes. Some have petals that are elegantly twisted, while others are marked with hairs and warts. All slipper orchids are noted for very-long-lasting blooms — the flowers usually last six to eight weeks. Many slipper orchids have gorgeous marbled foliage, which makes them stunningly beautiful, even when they aren't in bloom. Collectors of slipper orchids tend to be a fanatic lot — and it's easy to see why.

The official name of this group is *Paphiopedilum* 'Asian Lady's Slipper,' but you'll probably hear them referred to as lady's slippers or just plain slipper orchids — though they're anything but plain. These orchids got their common name because of their pouchlike lip, or *labellum,* which resembles a lady's slipper (see Figure 12-1).

In this chapter, I introduce you to the world of lady's slipper orchids — giving you some slipper-specific growing tips, some suggestions of varieties to buy, and some tips on which hybrids are your best bet.

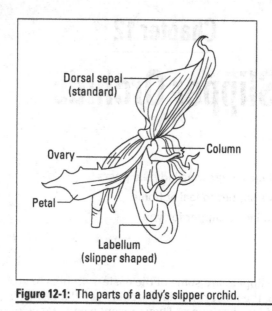

Dorsal sepal (standard)

Ovary

Column

Petal

Labellum (slipper shaped)

**Figure 12-1:** The parts of a lady's slipper orchid.

# Slipping into a Lady's Slipper

Lady's slippers are wonderful flowers for beginning orchid growers. In this section, I fill you in on why you should consider growing one, what kind of environment to give a lady's slipper after you bring it home, and how best to encourage your lady's slipper to bloom.

## Seeing what lady's slippers have to offer

Lady's slippers are extremely popular among orchid growers — professional and amateur alike — because

- ✔ They display a great diversity of flower forms.
- ✔ Many are easy to grow.
- ✔ Many have beautiful foliage.
- ✔ Most have very-long-lasting flowers, usually lasting many weeks.

## Giving your lady's slipper a good home

Although lady's slipper orchids are found in cold climates in North America, the ones that are most commonly grown indoors are the ones from the old-world tropics, like Southeast Asia. Almost all lady's slippers grow well in average home temperatures — 65°F to 75°F (18°C to 24°C) during the day, and 55°F to 60°F (13°C to 18°C) during the evening — and have modest humidity requirements.

Some of the lady's slippers are among the least demanding orchids when it comes to light, so they're very adaptable to growing on windowsills or under lights. (For more general orchid-growing details, check out Chapter 5.)

## Getting lady's slippers to bloom

Slipper orchids are some of the easiest of all orchids to grow and bloom. That said, you can't force these plants to flower if they're not mature or if it isn't their normal time of year to bloom. If your slipper orchid hasn't bloomed in over a year, and it needs a little nudging, try this three-step method:

1. **Grow your lady's slipper in a little brighter spot (see Chapter 5 for more details about orchid light needs).**

   If you don't see the flower buds forming in six to eight weeks, keep it in this same location and move to Step 2.

2. **Drop the temperature at night about 20°F (12°C) cooler than the daytime temperature.**

   If you don't see buds forming in six to eight weeks, move it back to its regular growing temperature and then move to Step 3.

3. **Let your lady's slipper get a little drier than usual for six to eight weeks.**

# Straight from Nature: Bumps, Warts, Hairs, and All

Lady's slipper *species,* which is what the plants are called as they come from the wild, display an exotic array of nature's work. In the following sections, I give you a sampling of some of the easier-to-grow of the more than 60 commonly found lady's slipper species.

## Paphiopedilum bellatulum

*Paphiopedilum bellatulum* is not the easiest of all lady's slippers, but it isn't difficult if you just keep in mind that these plants prefer to be a little cooler and drier than the other lady's slippers.

This orchid is commonly called the "egg-in-a-nest orchid," because that's what its white pouch looks like as it's surrounded by its rounded-white with burgundy-spotted petals. The thick leaves of this dwarf grower (only a few inches high) are beautifully patterned (see Figure 12-2).

**Figure 12-2:** *Paphiopedilum bellatulum* is a compact-growing horticultural gem.

## Paphiopedilum callosum

*Paphiopedilum callosum* was the first lady's slipper orchid that I grew, over 30 years ago. I had imported it from Thailand, and seeing it bloom for the first time was a thrill! It continued to perform on a regular basis.

This orchid is one of the simplest to grow and one of the most dependable to bloom. It comes in various flower shapes and color combinations of burgundy and green (see Figure 12-3). Its strong constitution and attractiveness make it very popular as a parent in hybridizing. This species is quick to multiply, so it'll give you a large plant in a relatively short time.

**Figure 12-3:** *Paphiopedilum callosum* is as dependable a bloomer as you can find.

## *Paphiopedilum delenatii*

*Paphiopedilum delenatii* is a delicate-looking, prized beauty. I used to find this orchid a bit on the temperamental side when it came to growing. Fortunately, the newer forms on the market today have more vigor and aren't finicky as they once were. Mine blooms dependably each spring, bearing one or two elegant light pink petal flowers with a darker pink pouch (see Figure 12-4). Unlike most lady's slippers that are scentless, this one possesses a subtle and delightful citrus fragrance.

## *Paphiopedilum dianthum*

*Paphiopedilum dianthum* is a Chinese species that is relatively easy to grow, needing just a modest amount of light — mine blooms consistently every year. This orchid puts on a floral display for many weeks. Its flowers have twisted green petals and a burgundy-brown pouch, topped with a white dorsal. The 12- to 16-inch (30- to 40-cm) leaves of this slipper orchid are glossy green with a leathery texture (see Figure 12-5).

## *Paphiopedilum fairrieanum*

The upswept petals and prominently marked dorsal of the *Paphiopedilum fairrieanum* present an exotic display (see

Figure 12-6). This is another slipper orchid that is undemanding and can be quickly grown into a nice-sized plant. The most common form of this species has petals striped in greens and purples, but there are other color combinations that are yellow, dark red, and green —some have longer and narrower petals than the standard type. The albino form — green and white — is especially enchanting.

**Figure 12-4:** *Paphiopedilum delenatii* displays special elegance.

**Figure 12-5:** *Paphiopedilum dianthum* requires a very modest amount of light to grow and flower well.

## A conservation success story

The history of the discovery and collection of orchids is littered with dismaying accounts of man's destruction of habitats resulting from the careless and greedy collection of these plants from their native lands. Encouragingly, this isn't always the case.

*Paphiopedilum delenatii* was first discovered in Vietnam in 1913 by a French officer. From the plants collected and exported at that time, only a few survived. One of them was grown by the famous French orchid nursery of Marcel Lecoufle, who successfully produced seeds from it. Shortly after, no more of the plants of this species were able to be found in the wild. For generations, all the plants of *Paphiopedilum delenatii* that were known were those resulting from these seedlings form Marcel Lecoufle!

Now this is a commonly grown and admired species.

**Figure 12-6:** *Paphiopedilum fairrieanum* hails from the cliffs of India and Bhutan.

---

## An orchid with a history of intrigue

For over 50 years during the late 1800s and early 1900s, the source of this treasured orchid, *Paphiopedilum fairrieanum,* remained a mystery. The only plant that was known had shown up in a shipment of unknown origin. In 1904, the famous orchid purveyor in England, Frederick Sander, offered a reward of £1,000 for anyone leading to the rediscovery of this orchid. This bounty was enough to bring results as new plants were discovered and exported from Bhutan and sold in the English orchid auctions for princely sums. Now this same horticultural gem is commonly available for indoor gardeners worldwide to enjoy at a very modest price.

---

Keeping the plant on the cooler, dryer side for six weeks during the winter will encourage it to put on its spring flower show.

## *Paphiopedilum glaucophyllum*

*Paphiopedilum glaucophyllum* rewards you with a very long blooming period — its flowers open one at a time, so the plant can be in bloom for months. It has attractive blue-green foliage. Its fuzzy petals — green dorsal edged in white — and rosy pink pouch make quite a nice presentation (see Figure 12-7).

**Figure 12-7:** *Paphiopedilum glaucophyllum* is easy to grow and will reward you with months of bloom.

# *Paphiopedilum hirsutissimum*

*Paphiopedilum hirsutissimum* is another distinctive Asian beauty. It has long, lance-shaped, light-green foliage with purple-and-green-marked flowers with wavy edges (see Figure 12-8). It's a vigorous grower but can sometimes be a reluctant bloomer.

Some growers have found if they drop the night temperature to 40°F to 45°F (4°C to 7°C) for several weeks in early winter, this may trigger flowering.

**Figure 12-8:** *Paphiopedilum hirsutissimum* grows in cooler spots than many of the other slipper orchids.

# *Paphiopedilum spicerianum*

Definitely one of my favorites, *Paphiopedilum spicerianum* puts on a dramatic display. Its shining white dorsal marked with a purple vertical strip up its center, surrounded by the shades of green and brown on its petals and pouch, make it a showstopper. Its white dorsal is so special that this slipper has been used frequently as a parent in breeding to impart this beautiful feature to its progeny. Turn to the color photographs in the center of this book for an example of *Paphiopedilum spicerianum*.

# *Paphiopedilum sukhakulii*

Some commercial growers lament that *Paphiopedilum sukhakulii* grows so quickly that they can't keep up with it. This is a "problem" that most amateur orchid growers would *love* to have! *Paphiopedilum sukhakulii* is a compact grower with prominently and attractively marked foliage. Figure 12-9 illustrates my plant in a 4-inch (8-cm) pot.

Its flowers offer a green-and-white-striped dorsal, wide-horizontal petals that are green with mahogany spots and sprinkled with warts and hairs, all set off with a dark maroon pouch. This species quickly forms a good-sized plant with many leads, and it frequently blooms more than once a year. See the color photographs in the center of this book for another example.

**Figure 12-9:** *Paphiopedilum sukhakulii* is a compact-growing, undemanding, high-performing slipper orchid.

## *Paphiopedilum venustum*

Described in the early 1800s, *Paphiopedilum venustum* was the first of the lady's slippers to be cultivated. Its handsome foliage makes it a standout even before its flowers, with distinctly veined lips and brightly colored petals, put on their show (see Figure 12-10). *Paphiopedilum venustum* is found in many different color forms.

Letting the plants get a little drier in the winter than you would in the summer increases their likelihood of flowering.

**Figure 12-10:** *Paphiopedilum venustum* is easily identified by its prominently veined lip or pouch.

# One Step Removed from Nature: Primary Hybrids

Primary hybrids are the results of *crossing* (mating) two different species, like the ones mentioned in the preceding sections, to create a new plant. In doing this, exciting new forms of orchids are created. The crossing process started in the 1800s and is continuing at full speed today. As new species are being discovered or better forms of the same species are showing up, the orchid breeder gets more new genetic material to play with. The results of some of these efforts are quite impressive.

The goals of breeding vary within the group, but the main purpose is to

✔ Expand the color range.

✔ Vary the flower shapes.

✔ Make the flowers larger.

✔ Create a new "look."

✔ Make the plants more compact.

✔ Make the plants more vigorous and easier to bloom.

In the following sections, I introduce you to just a handful of some of the many great successes. It's fun to look at the parents and guess what the offspring will look like. There are plenty of surprises!

## Some superior primary hybrids

These primary hybrids do their parents proud! Each of the following hybrids carries the good looks from its parents, but also adds its own new beauty and, in most cases, is more vigorous and easier to grow than either of the parents:

- ✒ *Paphiopedilum* **Angela:** From the photo of this variety (see Figure 12-11), can you take a guess what one of its parents is? Do you see the exotic touch from one of its parents, *Paphiopedilum fairrieanum* (refer to Figure 12-6)? Its other parent is a darling white species that can be a bit difficult to grow well, *Paphiopedilum niveum.* When these two are mated, the offspring — *Paphiopedilum* Angela — is a delightful compact-growing plant, easier to grow like *Paphiopedilum fairrieanum,* but with the delicate white coloring from *Paphiopedilum niveum.*

- ✒ *Paphiopedilum* **Armeni White:** Another good choice, this hybrid has very-dark-green patterned foliage and a large, soft-white flower.

- ✒ *Paphiopedilum* **Delophylum:** This is an enchanting orchid with soft pink flowers, borne sequentially, on compact plants with attractively marked foliage.

**Figure 12-11:** *Paphiopedilum* Angela has a charming flower on a compact plant.

✓ *Paphiopedilum* **Fumi's Delight:** This is another case where two fetching but sometimes-tricky-to-grow species, when mated or crossed, yield a more vigorous offspring than either of the parents. One parent has a bright yellow flower *(Paphiopedilum armeniacum);* the other *(Paphiopedilum micranthum)* has a pink bloom. The offspring of these parents have flowers varying in color from creamy yellow to light pink (see Figure 12-12).

✓ *Paphiopedilum* **Ho Chi Minh:** This is a new hybrid that is highly sought after. One of its parents is *Paphiopedilum vietnamense,* a gorgeous dark pink slipper recently discovered, and the other is *Paphiopedilum delenatii,* an elegant soft pink flowered slipper (refer to Figure 12-4). This should be a winning match.

✓ *Paphiopedilum* **Gloria Naugle:** This orchid is the result of crossing the largest-flowered and king of the slippers, *Paphiopedilum rothschildianum,* with *Paphiopedilum micranthum.* This hybrid inherits the bold stripes from *Paphiopedilum rothschildianum* and the hot pink from its other parent. The results are quite striking (see Figure 12-13).

✓ *Paphiopedilum* **Magic Lantern:** One of the most popular newer primaries, Magic Lantern, is a dependable grower and bloomer and its dark pink to red-pink flowers always elicit *oohs* and *ahs.*

**Figure 12-12:** *Paphiopedilum* Fumi's Delight is a popular primary hybrid.

**Figure 12-13:** *Paphiopedilum* Gloria Naugle presents an arresting picture.

- ✓ *Paphiopedilum* **Makulii:** Although not literately a primary, this orchid is very close to it. This hybrid takes the dramatic petal markings from *Paphiopedilum sukhakulii* (refer to Figure 12-9) and combines them with the darker flower colorations of its Maudiae hybrid cousins (see the section "Marvelous Maudiaes," later in this chapter). This lady's slipper is a snap to grow.

- ✓ *Paphiopedilum* **Saint Swithin:** Another hybrid — with one of its parents being the huge *Paphiopedilum rothschildianum* — this orchid is combined with another impressive bloomer, *Paphiopedilum philippinense,* which has a smaller growth habit and a history of being easier to flower. The result is striped flowers with dangling twisted petals — nothing less than extraordinary (see Figure 12-14). This is a larger lady's slipper than some of the others, but it's well worth the growing space! This one does require more light that the other slippers mentioned earlier. Grow in the same medium to bright light you provide cattleyas and it will be happy.

- ✓ *Paphiopedilum* **Transvaal:** This is a classic beauty first bred in 1901 and still popular today. It takes its stateliness from *Paphiopedilum rothschildianum* but reduces its size and adds ease of blooming from its other parent, *Paphiopedilum chamberlainianum.* This is another orchid that likes it bright, like Saint Swithin.

- ✓ *Paphiopedilum* **Vanda M. Pearman:** One of the most popular of all primary hybrids, Vanda M. Pearman has large light pink flowers dusted with dark burgundy spots, all shown off against thick, leathery, gorgeously marbled foliage (see Figure 12-15). This is a must-have lady's slipper.

Photograph courtesy of Marc Herzog

**Figure 12-14:** *Paphiopedilum* Saint Swithin puts on a spectacular show!

**Figure 12-15:** *Paphiopedilum* Vanda M. Pearman is admired for its elegant flower and attractive foliage.

## Marvelous Maudiaes

What a fabulous group of lady's slippers these are. The word *Maudiae* is the name given to one of the first hybrids made, in 1901, between *Paphiopedilum callosum* (see the color photographs in the center of this book for an example) and *Paphiopedilum lawrenceanum. Paphiopedilum* Maudiae and its offspring are noted for their exceptional vigor, ease of blooming (sometimes more than once a year), undemanding growing requirements, gorgeous foliage, and striking, gloriously colored flowers. They are found in three major color groups or combinations, covered in the following sections.

### Green-and-whites

Green-and-white Maudiaes are occasionally referred to as *albinos* because they lack the more commonly found red pigment. There is a simple timeless elegance to these flowers. They're highly revered in Europe as cut flowers.

Some super clones exist within this group like *Paphiopedilum* Claire de Lune 'Edgard van Belle' AM/AOS (see Figure 12-16). Its regal name fits its aristocratic look. It's huge impressive flower stands proudly above dark green handsome foliage. I received a division of this plant from a now deceased dear friend, Frances Nelson. It's a treasured memory of him, and I've shared divisions of it with special friends. It's a vigorous grower that still wins ribbons for me at orchid shows.

Another famous clone is *Paphiopedilum* Maudiae 'The Queen' AM/AOS. If you're fortunate to find these clones at a price you can live with, snatch them up. If they're too pricey for you at this point, try any of the standard green-and-white Maudiaes. None of them will disappoint you.

**Figure 12-16:** *Paphiopedilum* Claire de Lune 'Edgard van Belle' AM/AOS is a prize for anyone's orchid collection.

### Coloratums

This group is typified by a large dorsal and petals displaying streaks of purple in the flowers. The flower shape of this type looks very similar to the green-and-white Maudiae but has much more red and burgundy markings (see Figure 12-17). Many times the dorsal is larger and rounder.

**Figure 12-17:** A coloratum type. Notice the wide dorsal and the streaks of darker color throughout the flower.

### Vinicolors

The flowers of this type look like they've been varnished. They're a rich dark red or purple and have many admirers. This is probably the most sought after form of the Maudiae types. Their solid burgundy to mahogany blossoms shine (see Figure 12-18).

There are many good vinicolor varieties out there — too many to list. If you're lucky enough to actually see them in bloom, you can choose the ones that you like best. Unfortunately, because they're popular and are quickly snatched up, you may be forced to pick out blooming-size plants or ones in bud so you aren't sure what they'll look like when they bloom.

Here are two ways to increase your odds for buying the best:

 ✓ **Check out their parents.** Several orchid parents have a good reputation for producing high-quality offspring. Here are some to look for:

  • Black Cherry

  • Blood Clot (Ugh! What a name!)

- Eric Meng

- Laser

- Macabre

- Raisin Pie

- Red Fusion

- Red Glory

- Ruby Peacock

✔ **Look at the color of the leaves, flower stem, and bud.** The darker the purple in the newest leaves, the undersides of the leaves, the flower stem, and the buds, the greater the likelihood that the flower will also carry this dark pigment.

**Figure 12-18:** A vinicolor showing solid dark coloration over the entire flower.

## *Huge and round: Modern hybrid lady's slippers*

These lady's slippers are sometimes called "bulldogs" or "toads." To tell you the truth, I don't know how they got branded with such odd nicknames! They look nothing like these two creatures to me.

Another moniker for them is *complex hybrids,* and this makes sense, because their parentage is very convoluted, many times consisting of 20 or more parents.

All the orchids in this group have plain green foliage and most of their flowers are huge and round (see Figure 12-19). They're basically categorized by their flower colors: spotted, green, white, yellow, red, pink, and shades of these colors. A spotted one of mine that has been a delight is *Paphiopedilum* Langley Pride 'Burlingame' HCC/AOS (see the color photographs in the center of this book for an illustration).

**Figure 12-19:** A modern complex hybrid showing its full, round flower.

The whites have been particularly elusive in this quest for perfection. An older hybrid, *Paphiopedilum* F.C. Puddle (see Figure 12-20), doesn't match many of today's hybrids in terms of size and shape but is still in many collections today because it's a charming dependable grower and bloomer.

## A different kind of slipper orchid

All the slipper orchids that I cover up to this point in this chapter are tropical ones found in the old-world tropics, mostly various parts of Asia. Another type of lady's slipper has been known about since the 1800s but is now witnessing a strong new interest by orchid lovers. This group is called phragmipediums or simply "phrags."

Phragmipediums call their home Central and South America. Many grow in the mountains, and number more than 30 species. They have a similar growth habit to some of the paphiopedilums and have the same requirements for humidity and temperatures.

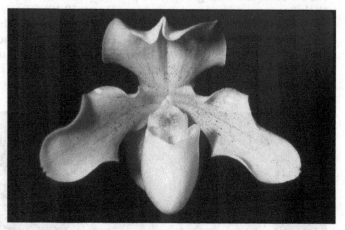

**Figure 12-20:** *Paphiopedilum* F.C. Puddle is an older white hybrid still appreciated today.

Culturally, they have some differences. In general, they like it wetter than paphiopedilums. In fact, they're commonly grown in platters of fresh water. This practice is unheard of with most other orchids! Also, they prefer more light — similar to cattleyas. These used to be expensive plants, but their prices have come down thanks, in part, to Hawaiian growers who have perfected their culture so they can now be grown to selling-size plants in record-breaking time.

Most of the flowers are twisted and dangling, are borne sequentially, and are found in shades and stripes of green and maroon. However, there are some key exceptions. *Phragmipedium besseae* is bright red-orange to yellow, *Phragmipedium xerophyticum* is white with a touch of pink, and *Phragmipedium schlimii* (see Figure 12-21 for a hybrid of this species) is a shade of pink as is *Phragmipedium fischeri*. But the absolute star of the show is a recently discovered marvel, *Phragmipedium kovachii,* with immense 7- to 8-inch (17.5- to 20-cm) magenta flowers. (See the nearby sidebar for more on this special plant.)

Although there has always been interest in the phragmipedium species, it is the hybrids that everyone its talking about. These newer hybrids are more vigorous and easy growing then most of the species and are becoming available in a broad range of colors. Many new ones are on the horizon but here are a few to look out for:

- ✔ *Phragmipedium* **Andean Fire** has attractive dark red 3½-inch flowers on tall flowering stems.

- ✔ *Phragmipedium* **Cardinale** is a classic hybrid that reliably produces many pink flowers.

- ✔ *Phragmipedium* **Hanne Popow** has delightful small pink flowers and is an old favorite that is still offered and is frequently used as a parent to produce newer hybrids.

- ✔ *Phragmipedium* **Jason Fischer** has eye-popping brilliant, broad, flat red flowers.

- ✔ *Phragmipedium* **Les Dirouilles** displays huge, spectacular green, chestnut, and burgundy flowers with long, twisted petals.

- ✔ *Phragmipedium* **Sorcerer's Apprentice** has broad foliage with very large and dramatic flowers with twisted petals in shades of green, brown, and burgundy.

**Figure 12-21:** *Phragmipedium* 'Wilcox' AM/AOS is a lovely hybrid with a delicate beauty.

# New Phrag creates a scandal!

*Phragmipedium kovachii* was "discovered" in 2002 at a roadside vendor in northeast Peru by an American orchid enthusiast, J. Michael Kovach. He immediately recognized it as being exceptional and probably new to the orchid world. Kovach purchased this rare orchid and pirated it back to the United States, illegally, with grand visions of his name entering the annals of orchid history by having this "holy grail of orchids" named after him.

He rushed it to the orchid experts at Selby Botanical Garden, one of the world's leaders in orchid research, to get it identified, documented, and officially described in Latin so it could be published in a botanical journal, thereby assuring that the orchid would be his namesake.

Now the fly in the ointment — the feds. They got word of Kovach's "discovery" and orchids hit the fan. Kovach was indicted, and they threatened to fine Selby Botanical Gardens $100,000 (it was plea-bargained to $5,000 and three years' probation). Selby botanists, administrators, and board members' heads rolled.

Even though it was part of the plea bargain that the name of this orchid be reverted to an earlier proposed name, *Phragmipedium peruviana,* most orchid people think it will most likely never happen.

And the scandal goes on. In the spring of 2004 at a Miami orchid show, a vendor and orchid grower from Peru, along with another orchid vendor and grower from Texas, were arrested for selling and smuggling endangered orchids including plants of *Phragmipedium kovachii.*

So, as you can see, orchid mania is alive and well today.

# Chapter 13

# Dancing Ladies: Oncidiums and Their Relatives

*T*his group of orchids is referred to as "dancing ladies" because the lips of many of them are flared like a flounced dancing gown, and the tops of the flowers, with a little imagination, look like the arms and head of a person.

Oncidiums are a joyful bunch of orchids that frequently display a flurry of flowers in the sunny yellow to orange and brown color range, although there are some in shades of pink, red, and green. They've been popular since they were first introduced into England from South America in the late 1700s.

## Taking a Closer Look at the Ladies

Hundreds of oncidiums are in existence, but just a handful are grown with regularity today. In general, they can be grown in the same conditions as cattleyas (see Chapter 5 for more details).

### Oncidiums from the wild

Many oncidiums from the wild are used in producing hybrids (see the following section, "Hybrid oncidiums"). Here are a few species, among the many that are worth looking for:

✔ *Oncidium amplicatum* (see **Figure 13-1**): When this orchid is in full bloom in the summer, it displays a shower of 1-inch (2.5-cm) brilliant yellow flowers on sprays up to 4 feet (120 cm) long. The pseudobulbs are short and circular and are sometimes referred to as being turtle-shaped.

✔ *Oncidium cheirophorum:* This dwarf-growing oncidium (it matures to about 3 inches [7.5 cm]) has ½-inch (1.25-cm) bright yellow citrus-scented flowers on an arching spray.

✔ *Oncidium crispum:* A quite attractive oncidium with 3-inch (8-cm) rust red flowers and lips with yellow and orange markings on the lips. The flowers are borne on a long spray and its leaves get to be about 6 to 8 inches (15 to 20 cm) long. Its flowers have a musty scent.

✔ *Oncidium lanceanum:* Referred to as a "mule-leaf" orchid because its stiff leathery foliage takes on this shape, it has flat, long-lasting 2- to 2½-inch (6-cm) flowers of contrasting brown and yellow with a purple and white lip. The plant grows about a foot (30 cm) tall and has a strong honey scent when the plant is in the sunlight.

✔ *Oncidium longipes* (see **Figure 13-2**): A dwarf-growing species from Brazil that blooms in the fall. Its cinnamon scented flowers are ¾ to 1 inch (2 to 3 cm) across with dark yellow to reddish brown sepals and petals and bright yellow lips. It frequently blooms twice a year.

**Figure 13-1:** *Oncidium amplicatum* can fill up a windowsill with its shower of flowers.

**Figure 13-2:** *Oncidium longipes* is a small-growing plant that is perfect for the windowsill.

✔ **Oncidium maculatum:** This is a handsome species with 3-inch (8-cm) honey-scented yellow flowers prominently marked with mahogany spots on an arched 20-inch (50-cm) flower spike. It blooms best if it's grown on the dry side during the winter.

✔ **Oncidium onustum (see Figure 13-3):** Clear yellow flowers about 1¼ inches (3 cm) wide cover this miniature plant when it's in bloom in the fall. It likes very bright light and should be grown on the dry side, especially right after flowering.

**Figure 13-3:** *Oncidium onustum* is a miniature grower with lemon yellow flowers.

✔ ***Oncidium ornithorhynchum:*** This is one of my favorites! It's a miniature, easy-to-grow, and easy-to-flower orchid and rewards you with scads of ¾-inch (1.5-cm) flowers with pink to lavender blooms that have a fresh vanilla fragrance. The plant only grows 8 to 10 inches (20 to 22.5 cm), so it's perfect for a windowsill or under lights. It frequently blooms a few times a year.

✔ ***Oncidium splendidum:*** This oncidium is splendid, indeed. From Guatemala and Honduras, this stately upright flower spike is 3 feet (1 meter) or more and is covered with 2- to 3-inch (5- to 7.5-cm) flowers that feature a broad bright yellow lip. Give this species a bright spot with plenty of growing room and let it dry off during the winter.

## Hybrid oncidiums

As is the case with the other orchids mentioned in this book, there are many hybrids of oncidiums. The orchid breeders have extended the color range and ease of blooming with these hybrids:

✔ ***Oncidium* Sharry Baby (see Figure 13-4):** This is one of the most popular orchids in the world! This particular variety out-sells all the other orchids. Why? The number-one reason is that it has a very strong fragrance of chocolate or vanilla. It also blooms more than once a year, often around Christmastime. A mature plant has hundreds of ½-inch (1.5-cm) yellow-overlaid-with-burgundy flowers with a flared white lip with purple markings. It's a bone-tough plant that will grow when others wimp out. My neighbor has one that I gave her and, with very little TLC, it performs dependably every year. This variety is available in many different color forms. As long as you have space for this one (it can grow over 30 inches [75 cm] tall), you can't go wrong buying one.

✔ ***Oncidium* Twinkles:** This is another star performer but with a quite different stature from Sharry Baby. It's parents, *Oncidium cheirophorum* and *Oncidium ornithrhynchum,* both mentioned earlier in this chapter, are fragrant and dwarf. The resultant crossing is a hybrid that is even better than its parents — more vigorous and free flowering. This one is highly recommended for beginners. It's available in various color forms.

✔ ***Oncidium* Tsiku Marguerite:** A very vigorous but small-growing (about 6 inches [15 cm] tall) hybrid that is sweet-scented. It produces densely branched sprays of ¾-inch (2-cm) cream to pink flowers. Another great beginner's orchid.

✔ ***Oncidium* Nathakhum:** This is a larger-growing oncidium with foliage up to about 12 inches (30 cm) long. It shows much influence from one of it parents, *Oncidium lanceanum,* with its mule-ear foliage and its flat, honey-scented, long-lasting flowers of contrasting brown and yellow with a yellow lip.

**Figure 13-4:** *Oncidium* Sharry Baby is a fast and easy growing and blooming *Oncidium* hybrid with the fragrance of chocolate.

## Miniature oncidiums or tolumnia

Until fairly recently, the miniature plants that look very much like oncidiums were called *equitant* (or *variegata*). Plant *taxonomists* (people who name plants) are now in a huddle to decide whether or not these plants should be assigned to the genus *tolumnia* rather than *oncidium*.

Whatever name you want to call them, they're darling little plants that are easy to grow. They have triangular thick leaves and are grown best in a sunny spot with good air movement. They're often mounted on wood or cork (see Chapter 7) but can also be grown in pots. Because they're small plants in small containers (see Figure 13-5), you must keep an eye on them so they don't dry out too severely.

Many of these orchids bloom a few times a year and will flower more than once on the same flower spike, so don't cut off the flower spike until it withers.

So many hybrids are available within this group that choosing one over another is difficult. Just look in the orchid suppliers' catalogs, on their Web sites, or in their greenhouses in the miniature orchid or miniature oncidium or tolumnia section. They're all easy growers and prolific bloomers (see Figure 13-6).

**Figure 13-5:** Equitant oncidiums require little space to grow and bloom. This one is in a 3-inch pot.

**Figure 13-6:** Even though the equitants are small plants, they have quite a bit of flower power, as this pink and red hybrid proves.

## One person's weed is another's treasure

Goodale Moir is a well-known name in the annals of orchid breeding. He dared to love a group of oncidiums called *equitants* or *variegata oncidiums*. At the time, in the 1950s, many of his less-enlightened orchid-breeding friends derided these miniatures from the Caribbean as "weeds." This didn't stop Goodale from pursuing his dream of breeding and developing these lovelies into small orchids of all colors and shades. While I was working at a botanical garden in Hawaii, in the 1970s, I was fortunate enough to meet him and his lovely wife, May, as his work was starting to be appreciated. Sadly, today, Goodale is no longer with us, but he left behind his proud legacy of these miniature horticultural gems.

# Pansy Orchids: Miltonias and Miltoniopsis

To see these orchids in bloom is to want them. True to their name, many of these orchids do have pansylike faces, but they actually outdo the other garden plants with their colors and flower patterns. For some reason, these orchids haven't gotten their due attention for many years. They had a reputation for being difficult to grow. Most of the newer selections and hybrids are more vigorous, easy, and worth your effort to try.

It used to be that all the orchids in this group were called miltonias, but now most go by miltoniopsis. For more details on this name game, see the nearby sidebar.

These orchids have a flower structure similar to oncidiums. Figure 13-7 shows the miltonia flower structure.

Here are some guidelines that will help you have more success with these beauties:

- ✔ **Miltonias like it a little warmer than miltoniopsis.** Miltonias like it up to about 84°F (29°C) during the day and around 55°F (12.8°C) during the evening. Miltoniopsis like it about 5°F to 10°F cooler for day and night temperatures.

- ✔ **Keep their roots damp but not wet.** Their fine root systems can easily be damaged by drying out. The catch-22 is that they can also be very susceptible to rotting if kept too wet. Use a fine-textured, well-drained potting material that also retains moisture.

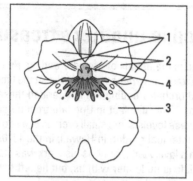

**Figure 13-7:** Miltonia flower structure:
1 = Sepals; 2 = Petals; 3 = Lip; 4 = Column.

✔ **If the leaves pucker in an accordion pattern, this is a sign the plant is not getting enough moisture.**

✔ **Keep these plants in small pots.** This is an easy way to prevent overwatering.

✔ **If the leaves are light green and standing upright, they're getting just the right amount of light.** If they're floppy and dark green, they're getting too little light. If they have a reddish cast, they're getting too much light.

✔ **Provide ample air circulation.** Otherwise, their thin leaves will get leaf spots from fungal disease.

## Miltonias

Here are a few miltonias that are particularly striking and easy to grow:

✔ *Miltonia flavescens:* The light yellow color of the flower sets this species off from the other miltonias. Its flowers are about 3 inches (7.5 cm) across and have a white lip with red spots.

✔ *Miltonia regnellii:* This is one of the most adaptable so it's one of the easiest of the miltonias to grow and bloom. For each erect stem, it has up to six white flowers that are about 2½ to 3 inches (6 to 7.5 cm) across with a purple-blue lip. It blooms in the summer to fall and has an orangelike fragrance.

✔ *Miltonia spectabilis:* One of the most popular and commonly offered miltonia species, it displays 4-inch-wide (10-cm-wide) flowers that are white tinged with pink. The lip is rose-pink with a purple column. This orchid grows to about 10 inches (25 cm) high and its flowers have a rosy fragrance. Another botanical variety, *Miltonia spectabilis* var. *moreliana,* has flowers of the same size but its sepals and petals are dark plum red with a contrasting large, bright rose-pink lip with darker veins. It is quite a looker!

✔ *Miltonia* **Goodale Moir:** A classic variety that is a namesake of a famous orchid breeder who lived in Hawaii, this miltonia hybrid likes warmer growing conditions and bears striking flowers with yellow petals spotted in burgundy and white lips brushed with a purple pink. *Miltonia* Goodale Moir is still frequently used as a parent to produce other warmth-loving miltonia hybrids.

✔ *Miltonia* **Anne Warne:** This is another time-proven, warmth-loving hybrid with gorgeous dark purple flowers with stunning purple-pink lips.

## Miltoniopsis

Some have said that that miltoniopsis can be more difficult to grow than miltonias, but it really matters which ones you get. Some species like it cooler and others tolerate warmer conditions. The hybrids seem to be very forgiving and easy. Many hybrids have spectacular markings, like the newer one shown in Figure 13-8.

**Figure 13-8:** A white miltoniopsis hybrid with striking purple markings.

## You say miltonia; I say miltoniopsis

The technical difference between these two is that all those orchids called miltonias have two, light green leaves per pseudobulb and "ears" on the column, in the center part of the flower. Miltoniopsis have one blue-green leaf per pseudobulb. Unless you're a taxonomist, the flowers look the same.

From a cultural point of view, miltonias are considered by some to be somewhat easier to grow because they're from Brazil, where it's warmer, while most of the miltoniopsis are from the cooler climes of Peru, Columbia, and Costa Rica so they can be more temperamental.

Here are some others that should be on your list:

✔ *Miltoniopsis phalaenopsis:* This species is the one primarily responsible for the "waterfall" patterns in the lips of today's hybrids. It likes warm summers and cool winters and does best if it's kept on the dry side during the winter. Its flower, which has the perfume of lily of the valley, is 1¾ inches (4 cm) and white pansy-shaped with a purple waterfall pattern on the lip. The plant reaches about 6 to 12 inches (15 to 30 cm) high.

✔ *Miltoniopsis roezlii:* A cool to warm grower, this is another one of the easier-to-grow miltoniopsis. It has 2½-inch-wide (6.5-cm-wide) white rose-scented flowers with dark-purple spots on each of the petals and a white lip with bright yellow and orange markings. The plant reaches about 9 inches (22 cm) tall.

✔ *Miltoniopsis santanaei* (see Figure 13-9): This is a very rewarding plant that is easy to grow and flower, which it often does more than once a year. Its flower is 2 inches (5 cm) wide, pristine white, flat, pansy-shaped with a bright yellow flare on the top of the lip. It's a compact-growing orchid — only 6 to 8 inches (15 to 20 cm) tall. It has a very sweet rose scent and is used frequently in breeding for this fragrant quality and its ease of culture.

✔ *Miltoniopsis* Bert Field: Pure velvety red, this hybrid's flowers are about 3 inches (7.5 cm) across. They're perfectly formed and some have waterfall patterns. It's a classic variety that is still found and is used often as a parent.

✔ *Miltoniopsis* Celle 'Wasserfall' (see Figure 13-10): There are many new hybrid miltonias, but this was one of the first to show such a spectacular "waterfall" pattern in the lip. Its red velvet sepals and petals and yellow column complete a gorgeous picture. The flowers have a rosy floral scent.

**Figure 13-9:** *Miltoniopsis santanaei* is a compact, easy-to-grow species well suited to growing on a windowsill or under lights.

**Figure 13-10:** Miltoniopsis Celle 'Wasserfall' is definitely a showstopper.

✔ *Miltoniopsis* **Hajime Ono:** Named after the noted Hawaiian miltoniopsis breeder, Hajime Ono, it has a magnificent 3½-inch-wide (9-cm-wide) dark-red velvety flower with a lip fantastically marked with a waterfall pattern. See the color section of photographs for an example.

✔ *Miltoniopsis* **Hamburg:** This is another famous cross that set the standard for quite a while for being one of the best of the solid reds. It has a light rosy fragrance.

# Other Members of the Club: The Oncidium Alliance

Many other orchids are related to oncidiums, and they're commonly referred to as being part of the Oncidium Alliance. In the following sections, I list some of the more prominent ones.

## Orchid spiders: Brassias

Large flowers with long, leggy petals and sepals typify this group of orchids. Although some of the species and hybrids of brassias are popular, they are more commonly used as parents with other oncidium relatives to pass on their elegant flower shapes (see "Mixing It Up," later in this chapter). Here are a few standouts of the 15 or so species of brassias:

- ✔ *Brassia longissima* (see Figure 13-11): This orchid features large spidery flowers about 7 to 8 inches (18 to 20 cm) from top to bottom that open greenish and turn orange over several days. The flowers are spotted maroon and have a sweet, candy scent. This is a tall grower that maxes out at about 30 inches (75 cm) tall.

- ✔ *Brassia maculata:* A commonly grown species, this orchid also follows the similar flower shape and color pattern of the other two species described in this list. It blooms in the summer and puts on a show of fragrant flowers for several weeks.

- ✔ *Brassia verrucosa:* Another spider-type flower that reaches about 6 to 8 inches (15 to 20 cm) across, this orchid is pale green and is spotted in darker green or brown with a white lip spotted with darker warts. This species is an easy one to grow. It has a musky scent.

## Butterfly orchids: Psychopsis

This orchid used to be called an oncidium and then was reclassified to this genus. It doesn't take much imagination to see how this orchid got its common name, butterfly orchid, because the flower looks very much like this regal insect.

*Psychopsis papilio* (shown in Figure 13-12) is the most popular species in the genus and is an easy one to grow, requiring the same cultural conditions as oncidiums. *Psychopsis papilio* has reddish leathery leaves with darker spots; its flowers have thin, dark burgundy, upright sepals that look like antennae; the petals are barred dark red on yellow; and the lip is yellow with solid or spotted burgundy red edging. Another species, *Psychopsis krameriana,* is very similar.

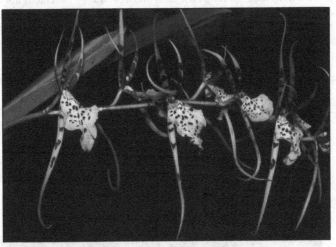

**Figure 13-11:** *Brassia longissima* is a fine selection of this species.

The flowers are borne in succession, so don't cut off the flower spike until it shrivels.

**Figure 13-12:** *Psychopsis papilio* has a butterfly look.

---

## Not for beginners

The Oncidium Alliance has other genera — including baptisonia, cochlioda, comparettia, odontoglossum, rodriguezia, and trichocentrum — but many are not noted for being easy to grow. Some are from cooler climates and require very high humidity. They have, however, played important roles as genetic building blocks to produce hybrids with all the other oncidium group. See the "Mixing It Up" section for more details.

---

## Sigmatostalix

*Sigmatostalix radicans* (shown in Figure 13-13) is a dainty and charming miniature orchid, reaching about 6 inches (15 cm). It has grasslike foliage and small ¾-inch (1 cm) white flowers with greenish sepals and petals with a brown column and white lip. Its flowers have a sweet honey fragrance.

*Photograph courtesy of Marc Herzog*

**Figure 13-13:** *Sigmatostalix radicans* is a miniature orchid with a honey scent.

---

## Trichopilia

Two orchids within the trichopilia genus are commonly grown:

✔ **Trichopilia suavis:** A native of Central and South America, this orchid has oblong pseudobulbs with leaves that can grow up to 16 inches (40 cm) long. It's frequently grown in a basket because the two to five fragrant flowers, white spotted with red, are borne on a pendulous flower spike. The lips of the flowers are tubular and have pink and orange spots.

✔ ***Trichopilia fragrans:*** This orchid is very similar to the preceding one and blooms in the spring to summer.

# Mixing It Up

Now things really get interesting! Imagine taking all the orchids that I introduce in this chapter from the Oncidium Alliance, and many more that I haven't even mentioned, and mating or breeding them with each other. This is just what has been done by skillful orchid breeders in the United States — and the results have been astounding!

Knowing where to begin is difficult, because there are so many different ones. By the late 1990s, almost 10,000 of these hybrids had been registered and breeding efforts have continued at full tilt, so today there are many more.

In general, these are orchids with wild color combinations and large flower counts that are durable, vigorous plants. These new hybrids are starting to compete with phalaenopsis for the public's favor.

These hybrids have a scrambled parentage. To help you sort through it all, Table 13-1 is a list of some of the most common and popular *intergeneric genera* (ones that have parents from more than one genus) along with the genera that were used to actually produce these new intergeneric genera. The abbreviations for the genera are also given, because this will usually be what you'll find written on the orchid label.

| Table 13-1 | Oncidium Alliance Intergenerics | |
|---|---|---|
| *Intergeneric Genus* | *Genera Used to Create This Genus* | *Abbreviation Used* |
| Aliceara | Brassia, Miltonia, Oncidium | Alcra. |
| Beallara | Brassia, Cochlioda, Miltonia, Odontoglossum | Bllra. |
| Brassada | Ada, Brassia | Brsa. |
| Brassidium | Brassia, Oncidium | Brsdm. |

*(continued)*

**Table 13-1 *(continued)***

| Intergeneric Genus | Genera Used to Create This Genus | Abbreviation Used |
|---|---|---|
| Burrageara | Cochlioda, Miltonia, Odontoglossum, Oncidium | Burr. |
| Colmanara | Miltonia, Odontoglossum, Oncidium | Colm. |
| Degarnoara | Brassia, Miltonia, Odontoglossum | Dgmra. |
| Milpasia | Miltonia, Aspasia | Mpsa. |
| Miltassia | Brassia, Miltonia | Mtssa. |
| Miltonidium | Miltonia, Oncidium | Mtdm. |
| Odontocidium | Odontoglossum, Oncidium | Odcm. |
| Odontonia | Odontoglossum, Miltonia | Odtna. |
| Rodricidium | Oncidium, Rodriguezia | Rdcm. |
| Vuylstekeara | Cochlioda, Miltonia, Odontoglossum | Vuyl. |
| Wilsonara | Cochlioda, Odontoglossum, Oncidium | Wils. |

Orchid breeders hybridizing these related orchids are working to impart the following qualities to their plants:

✔ More-compact growth and flowering habit

✔ Ease of flowering

✔ More tolerance for a wide range of growing temperatures

✔ Lower light requirements

✔ Blooming multiple times per year

✔ Bright, colorful patterns in the flowers

When you visit your orchid grower, check out orchid supplier Web sites, or go to orchid shows, you'll see that today's hybrids in this group are moving closer and closer to meeting these breeding objectives.

Because this group is so huge, I've tried to hit on some of the most popular in this group. This is only the tip of the iceberg:

✔ *Beallara* **Marfitch 'Howard's Dream' (see Figure 13-14):** This orchid has dazzling, large, deep burgundy flowers on upright flower spikes with white markings and a dash of yellow on the lip. These are always the plants people stop to admire at the orchid shows.

✔ **Beallara Tacoma Glacier:** This is found in various forms but most have very large frilly flowers with red markings.

✔ **Brassidium Fly Away 'Miami' HCC/AOS (see Figure 13-15):** These bright yellow flowers are borne in huge numbers and look like they are taking off in flight.

**Figure 13-14:** *Beallara* Marfitch 'Howard's Dream' is always the center of attention when it's in bloom.

**Figure 13-15:** The flowers of *Brassidium* Fly Away 'Miami' HCC/AOS have masses of flowers on long flower spikes.

✔ *Burrageara* **Stefan Isler:** This orchid has upright stems with many brilliant red flowers with a lighter color lip. It is free flowering and will bloom more than once a year when the plant is mature.

✔ *Colmanara* **Wildcat (see Figure 13-16):** There are many different selections of this orchid, but they are all very bright yellow, waxy flowers about 3 inches (7.5 cm) across with very distinct yellow or maroon markings, and a lip that is usually very dark red and marked with yellow. It's quite a standout.

**Figure 13-16:** *Colmanara* Wildcat has dramatic feline markings on a waxy long-lasting flower.

✔ *Degarnoara* **Winter Wonderland 'White Fantasy' (see Figure 13-17):** Many selections of this orchid are available, but they look very similar. They have large white flowers and lip with sepals that extend slightly backward. The lip and petal are lightly spotted in red. The flower is said to have the fragrance of bananas. An established plant will bloom a few times a year

✔ *Milpasia* **Milt's Choice 'Helen of Troy':** Long-lasting yellow with rose to maroon stripes on the petals with a large white lip are the features of this orchid. It grows about 10 to 12 inches (25 to 30 cm) tall and has a rosy fragrance.

✔ *Miltassia* **hybrids:** Most of this group are usually strongly marked and brightly colored. See the color section for an example.

✔ *Miltonidium* **Bartley Schwartz (see Figure 13-18):** Several different forms of this are available, but most have upright spikes of many red to purple flowers with white lips marked in red.

**Figure 13-17:** *Degarnoara* Winter Wonderland 'White Fantasy' has a unique blend of lip shape similar to miltonia, longer petals like brassia, and wider flowers like odontoglossum.

✔ *Miltonidium* **Issaku Nagata 'Volcano Queen' HCC/AOS:** An easy orchid with many 1½-inch (4-cm) flowers on tall multi-branched spikes. The petals and sepals are yellow overlaid with mahogany. The flared lip is white at the bottom and red and purple at the top. The foliage can grow 18 to 24 inches (45 to 60 cm) tall and the flowers have a light floral fragrance.

✔ *Odontioda* **Margarete Holm 'Alpine':** A gorgeous full-bodied white flower with clear burgundy markings. See the color section of photographs for an example.

✔ *Odontioda* **Vespa 'Charm' (see Figure 13-19):** This is a captivating, very compact orchid that only grows 6 to 8 inches (15 to 20 cm) tall. It displays 2½-inch (6.5-cm) white, citrus-scented flowers that are decorated with distinct purple and red markings on the petals and sepals with yellow on the throat. I love this one!

**Figure 13-18:** *Miltonidium* Bartley Schwartz comes in many forms, but all have many red to purple flowers on an upright flower spike.

**Figure 13-19:** *Odontioda* Vespa 'Charm' is a favorite because of its compact habit and colorful flower markings.

✔ ***Odontobrassia* Fangtastic Bob Henley:** Seventy-five percent of this hybrid's lineage is from brassias, so it has characteristically spidery yellow flowers that are 4 to 5 inches (10 to 13 cm) across with maroon markings and yellow lips on arching flower spikes.

- *Odontocidium* **Crowborough:** This hybrid is another one of the earlier crosses that is still available today and is used plenty as a parent for newer hybrids. It has 3-inch (7.5-cm), bright yellow, thick-textured flowers with distinct mahogany markings.

- *Odontocidium* **Tiger Crow 'Golden Girls' HCC/AOS:** An offspring of famous parents, *Odontocidium* Tiger Hambuhren and *Odontocidium* Crowborough, it shows off 2½-inch (6.5-cm) golden-yellow flowers with maroon spots and a bright yellow lip. The plant grows about 18 inches (45 cm) tall and the flowers have a light floral scent. See the color section of photographs for an example.

- *Vuylstekeara* **Cambria 'Plush' FCC/AOS (see Figure 13-20):** This is a classic variety and was one of the first of these intergenerics to hit the market in a big way. Its many flowers are a clear dark red, tipped in white with a red-and-white edge lip. This variety has stood the test of time.

**Figure 13-20:** *Vuylstekeara* Cambria 'Plush' FCC/AOS has proven itself to be a winner.

- *Vuylstekeara* **Yokara 'Perfection':** This is a dazzler! Its light burgundy flowers sparkle with bright white patterns throughout. A yellow highlight appears on the lip. See the color section for an example.

- *Wilsonara* **Tiger Brew:** A free flowering and branching plant that has flowers with sepals and petals that are light yellow and spotted with burgundy and a lip that is lemon yellow with reddish spots. The edges of the petals and sepals are touched in red and fringed.

# Chapter 14

# Significant Others

*In This Chapter*

▶ Discovering one of the biggest of all groups of orchids: Dendrobiums

▶ Finding orchids that are as weird as they get: Bulbophyllums

▶ Considering some other orchids

*I*n the previous chapters, I present you with some of the largest orchid groups that are most suitable for home orchid growing. But, as you can imagine, with tens of thousands of different orchids out there, some additional ones in other groups are also prime candidates. In this chapter, I give you a glimpse at some of them.

# A Huge and Interesting Lot: Dendrobiums

Dendrobiums and their close relatives number more than a thousand. They call their homes the old-world tropics, which include New Guinea and the exotic land down under, Australia. Some of these orchids have exacting cultural requirements that are a challenge to provide. The ones I show you here are the easier ones that have basically the same cultural requirements as cattleyas — medium to high light, modest humidity, and intermediate temperatures. Many of the dendrobiums naturally undergo a drier winter than summer, so they appreciate the same treatment from you. Some are *evergreen* (keeping their foliage year-round), while others are *deciduous* (dropping their leaves in the fall) as they enter a rest for the winter, then put out their new growth in the spring.

## The most popular dendrobiums

Here is a small selection of some of the easiest and most readily found dendrobiums that are not very demanding. As you become familiar with this huge group of plants, you'll surely find others you'd like to try out.

### Dendrobium phalaenopsis

Although the more proper name for this orchid is *Dendrobium bigibbum*, it rarely goes by this in the trade. I list this one first because it is by far the most popular and commonly found dendrobium. Luckily, it is also one of the least expensive and easiest to grow. Hybrids of this type are found in an impressive array of color combinations and are usually about 1½ to 3 inches (3 to 7 cm) across and look much like phalaenopsis flowers (thus, the species name of phalaenopsis). Figure 14-1 shows an example of a *Dendrobium phalaenopsis.* The most common flower colors are white, shades of pink, and purple, but some of the newer offerings have contrasting sepals, petals, and lips in a whole range of pastels.

**Figure 14-1:** The *Dendrobium phalaenopsis* flower looks much like a phalaenopsis orchid (see Chapter 10).

*Dendrobium phalaenopsis,* which are evergreens, differ dramatically in their growth habits — some are very compact, about 6 inches (15 cm) tall while others can reach 3 feet (1 meter) or more in height (see Figure 14-2).

Like most dendrobiums, the *Dendrobium phalaenopsis* prefers to be pot-bound, so it's content to stay in a small container. It requires a modest drying-off period during the winter and early spring to promote flowering. You can resume regular watering when new growth appears in the spring until after flowering.

*Dendrobium phalaenopsis* hybrids, sometimes referred to as "cane" Dendrobiums because of their upright stems, can vary tremendously in their growth habits from dwarfs to giants. Figure 14-2 shows one of the larger forms.

Figure 14-2: A larger *Dendrobium phalaenopsis* hybrid.

### Dendrobium nobile

Another one of the most popular dendrobiums, the *Dendrobium nobile* (shown in Figure 14-3) has been hybridized extensively so that today's varieties come in a carnival of bright colors.

The *Dendrobium nobile* is deciduous, so when winter approaches, keep it on the dry side. Only water it enough to keep its pseudo-bulbs from shriveling. Let the evening temperatures get down around 50°F to 55°F (10°C to 13°C).

Figure 14-3: *Dendrobium nobile* var. *virginale* is a white form of this popular dendrobium.

Some people have described the fragrance of these orchids as being like honey or musk during the day and mown hay at night.

## Dendrobium kingianum

This dendrobium is wonderfully tough — it can withstand temperatures down to 35°F (1.6°C) — and easy to grow, and it's just starting to get its due. This Australian native was once considered a "weed" among some orchid growers, because it is such a rapid grower. Now it's getting new respect as more people are becoming aware of how easy and forgiving it is to grow and bloom and as many new flower color forms are appearing.

The usual flower is small, up to about 1 to 1½ inches (2.5 to 4 cm), in shades of pink, borne in 8-inch (20-cm) sprays of about a dozen flowers (see Figure 14-4). The newer selections include dark purple, purple-blue, white, striped, and a whole range of combinations of these. This orchid varies considerable in its growth habit from a few inches (5 cm) to almost 16 inches (50 cm) tall.

This orchid has a range of fragrances from hyacinth to lilac to honey.

*Dendrobium kingianum* requires a dry, cool winter to bloom dependably. It's an evergreen orchid that has attractive compact, thick, dark green foliage. It readily forms *keikis* (baby plants); refer to Chapter 8 to see how to handle them.

**Figure 14-4:** *Dendrobium kingianum* has small crystalline flowers that are found in various shades of purple and pink.

# Some other Dendrobiums worth considering

After you've cut your teeth on the easier dendrobiums mentioned in the previous section, try some of these:

✔ **Dendrobium aggregatum:** This orchid and its cousin, *Dendrobium jenkensii* (shown in Figure 14-5) are dwarf plants that produce showers of 1-inch (2.5-cm) golden yellow, honey-scented flowers with broad, almost heart-shaped lips. The flowers appear in groups of two or three for *Dendrobium jenkensii,* more for *Dendrobium aggregatum,* in the spring. The pseudobulbs are small, 1 to 2 inches (2.5 to 5 cm). These plants are frequently grown on slabs and are best not transplanted or divided often. They make their most spectacular display when they become large-sized plants.

✔ **Dendrobium bellatulum:** This is another miniature plant only reaching about 4 inches (10 cm) tall with one to three 1½-inch (4-cm) white flowers with orange and red markings in the lip. The flowers have a fresh lemon fragrance.

✔ **Dendrobium chrysotoxum:** This orchid has butter-yellow, pineapple- or mango-scented, 1-inch (2.5-cm) flowers with fringed lips and a darker orange throat that are displayed on a 12-inch (30-cm) flower spike (see Figure 14-6). The plant is evergreen and a compact grower.

**Figure 14-5:** *Dendrobium jenkensii* is a miniature grower that blooms best if it's transplanted very infrequently.

**Figure 14-6:** *Dendrobium chrysotoxum* produces sprays of golden flowers with the scent of tropical fruit.

✔ ***Dendrobium loddigesii:*** This is a compact grower that reaches about 6 inches (15 cm) tall. It's covered in the spring with 2-inch (5-cm) light-pink flowers with light-yellow lips that last about three weeks. It has a rambling habit, so it's most suited for mounting on a slab (see Chapter 7 for more information).

✔ ***Dendrobium scabrilingue:*** This miniature, growing only 3 to 5 inches (8 to 15 cm) high, has been in bloom for me for months! Its starry white 1-inch (2.5-cm) flowers have a touch of light yellow in the center with a pleasant sweet fragrance that reminds me of the white paste we used to use in elementary school for our art projects.

✔ ***Dendrobium lawesii:*** This is a screamer from the jungles of New Guinea with 1-inch (2.5-cm) bright red-orange, waxy flowers, tipped in yellow that are borne on leafless stems. It's found in several color forms and its floral brilliance and sweet scent make it in high demand. It needs a drier rest period during the winter. See the color photographs in the center of this book for an example.

Thousands of dendrobium hybrids exist, but many of them are best suited for a very cool greenhouse. In the following list, I focus on a few that are particularly easy and are a reasonable size to handle:

✔ ***Dendrobium* André Millar (frequently misspelled "Miller"):** Exotic green 1½-inch (4-cm) flowers, with lips prominently veined in dark maroon, make this orchid a standout (see

Figure 14-7). It apparently comes in two forms: one very compact, about 6 to 8 inches (15 to 20 cm) tall, and the other about twice or more this height. So if plant size is important to you, be sure to ask which form you're buying.

**Figure 14-7:** *Dendrobium* André Millar has flowers that have an almost alien look.

✔ ***Dendrobium* Iki:** A great miniature that rarely grows higher than 7 inches (20 cm), this orchid has attractive dark green, glossy, evergreen foliage and charming 1-inch (2.5-cm) creamy white flowers with red and orange in the lip. It has the sweet fragrance of licorice.

✔ ***Dendrobium* Jesmond Gem:** This dendrobium is merely representative of the many new hybrids that are coming into the United States from Australia. They're usually tough plants that can survive temperatures approaching freezing and, in fact, will usually bloom best if given a very cold period in the neighborhood of 40°F to 49°F (4°C to 8°C). If you have a very cool bright spot, be on the lookout for these fine hybrids. Jesmond Gem has pristine white, 2-inch (5-cm) sweet-smelling flowers with purple specks on the lips and yellow stripes down the center of the lips. It grows about 18 inches (45 cm) tall.

# Weird and Wonderful Relatives: Bulbophyllum

One of the many great aspects of the orchid world is that, with their seemingly countless species and hybrids, there is an orchid out there that meets absolutely anyone's fancy! For those who pursue the bizarre, otherworldly, and sometimes malodorous, bulbophyllums fill the bill perfectly. You have to see (or smell) these oddities to believe that they could exist. Many are *carrion flowers,* ones that smell like rotting meat; this is to attract their primary pollinators, various types of flies. Here are a few of the outstanding ones that are not particularly difficult to grow:

- ✔ **Bulbophyllum beccarii:** Contrary to the other orchids in this book, this one is *very* difficult to grow, but I simply had to let you know about it because it is the "grande stinko" of the orchid world. This orchid is described as smelling like "100 dead elephants rotting in the sun." This is not one you want to have in your living room! It's considered to be one of the most spectacular bulbophyllums, if you can stand the stench. Its leaves grow up to 2 feet (60 cm), so it's usually grown mounted, and it has small brown flowers with a purple blush.

- ✔ **Bulbophyllum echinolabium:** Displaying a dramatic flower that can be 1 foot (30 cm) or more long, this bulbophyllum has a dark-cream flower with mahogany stripes. It's a compact grower of about 6 to 8 inches (10 to 15 cm) tall (see Figure 14-8).

- ✔ **Bulbophyllum odoratissimum:** A miniature bulbophyllum that grows to about 3 inches (8 cm), this orchid has petite flowers of a dozen or more. The flowers are yellow with a reddish brown lip and actually smell pleasant.

- ✔ **Bulbophyllum lobbii:** A jasmine-scented species, this orchid is referred to as the "Queen of Bulbophyllums." The 3- to 4-inch (7.5- to 10-cm) yellow flowers with purple mottling are borne singly. The leaves are spatula-shaped and about 12 inches (30 cm) long.

- ✔ **Bulbophyllum phalaenopsis:** This is another stinker. It has huge leaves up to 4 to 6 feet (120 to 180 cm) long, shaped like those of phalaenopsis (thus, the species name). Its flowers are dark red with yellow protuberances. This huge plant is really only happy in a greenhouse. See the "Being stinky has its rewards" sidebar for more information.

- ✔ **Bulbophyllum rothschildianum:** One of the most spectacular of the bulbophyllums, this orchid has five or six flowers in a cluster. Each flower is about 1 inch (2.5 cm) wide and 7 inches (17.5 cm) long. The flowers have yellow bases covered with dark red and darker maroon lips. The plants grow about 12 inches (30 cm) high (see Figure 14-9).

**Figure 14-8:** *Bulbophyllum echinolabium* has a 1-foot-long (30-cm-long) flower, which makes it one of the largest in the genus.

**Figure 14-9:** *Bulbophyllum rothschildianum* has one of the most magnificent flowers of all bulbophyllums.

## Being stinky has its rewards

At the highly prestigious 2004 New York International Orchid Show, a gigantic mounted specimen of *Bulbophyllum phalaenopsis* shared the top honor with one other orchid to be Co-Grand Champion and also received a Certificate of Cultural Excellence from The American Orchid Society. This plant was said to be valued at thousands of dollars!

# Orchid Miscellanea: All the Rest

Having to give the rest of these fascinating orchids such little coverage is a shame, but with so many orchids and so little space. . . . In the following sections, I give very brief introductions to some example plants in other genera that deserve your attention.

## Catasetum

Looking closely at the shape of its showy flowers, you can see how the catasetum got tagged with its common name: Monkey Goblet. Many hybrids of this orchid are available, and they're relatively easy to grow.

 Catasetums are *deciduous* orchids, which means they like to be watered and fertilized copiously when they're in active growth, and then kept on the dry side during the winter — stop watering for four to six weeks — until they start new growth in the spring.

 *Catasetum* Orchidglade was the first commercial catasetum hybrid. This selection has up to 15 2-inch (5-cm) creamy white, thick, waxy flowers that are covered with red freckles. It has a spicy fragrance and, like other catasetums, is usually grown in a basket. It prefers rapid drainage; the flowers are borne on pendulous sprays at the bottom of the plant (see Figure 14-10).

## Cochleanthes

This is a beguiling genus of orchids that is starting to get more exposure. Cochleanthes have very attractive glossy green foliage, usually bloom more than once a year, are easy to grow (preferring the same growing conditions as phalaenopsis), and have exotic flowers.

**Figure 14-10:** *Catasetum* Orchidglade has pendulous flowers and pleated foliage typical of catasetums.

*Cochleanthes amazonica* has white, 2-inch (5-cm), rose- or candy-scented flowers with vivid dark purple veins on the impressive flared lip. A hybrid of this species, called Amazing, has very similar, but somewhat larger flowers (see the color photographs in the center of this book for an example). The plant grows about 8 inches tall.

Be sure to keep the potting material damp or the leaves will become pleated.

*Cochleanthes discolor* is another fine species that has 2-inch (5-cm) cream-colored flowers with a mauve cupped lip. It grows about 8 inches (20 cm) tall and has a cedar or candy fragrance.

*Cochleanthes* Moliere is a hybrid of *Cochleanthes amazonica* and *Cochleanthes discolor*. It is a marriage with a spectacular result: 2-inch (5-cm) flowers with white petals tipped with pink, and a huge, contrasting, dramatic purple lip.

## Coelogyne

A genus of about 100 species found in Asia, coelogyne orchids are usually fragrant. Most of them do best in medium to high light in intermediate temperatures; some from mountainous areas like it cooler. Most of them grow and look best when they're permitted to grow to a large size, not divided.

*Coelogyne cristata* is one of the popular species of this group. It displays white, banana-scented flowers that are about 3 inches (8 cm) wide with a white lip with yellow markings.

Because of its rambling habit, *Coelogyne cristata* is best grown into a large plant in a basket or mounted (see Figure 14-11). *Coelogyne intermedia* has white fruity-scented flowers with a yellow throat and grows to about 8 inches (20 cm) tall. *Coelogyne intermedia* should be kept on the damp side, or the foliage will become pleated.

**Figure 14-11:** *Coelogyne cristata* makes a beautiful sight as a large, well-grown plant.

## Cymbidiums

Cymbidiums are popular as corsage orchids because they last for such a long time, even after they've been cut from the plant. Thanks to modern orchid breeding, these orchids are now available in a vast array of colors — some with markings on the lips, others with totally clear flowers and lips. The ones that most people are familiar with are the "standard" cymbidiums.

A full-size plant in complete flower is a jaw dropper. However, these plants can get 2 to 4 feet (60 to 120 cm) or more tall and wide — they're serious space hogs. Also, some of the standard varieties require very cool and bright conditions for them to perform at their best.

The most common complaint of amateur cymbidium growers is that the plants grow fine, but they don't flower. If this sounds familiar, you're probably giving your cymbidium too little light or not giving it the cool evening temperature of 45°F to 50°F (7°C to 10°C) that it needs in order to trigger the formation of flower buds.

Newer, more-compact plants with a warmer temperature tolerance are appearing all the time, so life for the hobbyist cymbidium lover is getting easier. These smaller plants are referred to as "miniature," but be aware that this is a relative term. "Miniature" cymbidiums still reach about 2 feet (60 cm) tall but can be managed in a 6- to 8-inch (15- to 20-cm) pot.

Standard cymbidium hybrids are very popular as outside orchids in mild areas like Southern California. They're grown successfully in many places as long as they have enough light, cool evenings, and space. The newer ones, such as *Cymbidium* Solana Rose (shown in Figure 14-12), have very full, round flowers.

**Figure 14-12:** *Cymbidium* Solana Rose is a soft pink standard variety that exemplifies the new hybrid cymbidiums with large round flowers in pastel shades.

*Cymbidium* Golden Elf is a 2½-inch (6-cm) clear bright-yellow-flowered miniature variety with four to six flowers per spike. Its size is more manageable for most home growers. This one can bloom several times a year and is more tolerant of warmth. The lightly rose-scented flowers last for about two weeks.

## Lycaste

A deciduous plant, lycaste orchids have pleated foliage and triangular flowers. Many of them have a tantalizing fragrance. They like good air circulation, cool evenings of 45°F to 55°F (7°C to 13°C), and frequent and heavy waterings during the summer growing season. They should be kept on the dry side during the winter.

*Lycaste* Aquilea 'Détente' FCC/AOS is a prize-winner with a 4-inch (10-cm) peachy colored flower that has a sweet floral fragrance.

*Lycaste aromatia* has sunny lemon yellow, cinnamon-scented, 2½-inch (6-cm) flowers borne in groups of up to 30 or 40 on a compact plant — all of which makes this easy-to-grow species very popular.

If *Lycaste aromatia* is grown in bright light, the flowers have a more intense color.

## Zygopetalum

Oh, what a heavenly fragrance these have! When only one flowering zygopetalum plant is in a room, it smells like a bed of hyacinths. Most of the zygopetalums have similar color markings — usually, green petals barred in dark maroon or brown with a very broad and prominent white lip with dark purple or pink (see Figure 14-13). They're easy to grow and perform well on an eastern or southern windowsill.

**Figure 14-13:** A zygopetalum hybrid with typical markings.

# Part IV
# The Part of Tens

"Before I show you the rest of 'Castle Dracula', let me show you my garden. It's a hobby with me. I do most of the work myself, however, Renfield helps keep the garden free of bugs."

## In this part . . .

*H*ere I target four of the most burning issues amateur orchidists frequently ask me: What are the easiest orchids to grow? What is the most common ways orchids are killed? What are the most frequently asked questions about orchids and their culture? Why don't my orchids bloom? In this part, I give you some straightforward answers to these sometimes perplexing questions and issues so your orchid growing will be smooth sailing.

I remember my father buying me my first orchid plant when we were on a family vacation in Florida. How exciting that moment was for me! It was rare in those days, 40 years ago, to find a place that sold orchid plants and supplies, unless you traveled to Florida or California. Most of the northern growers produced orchids for cut flowers, not as pot plants. With the relatively recent strong surge of interest in orchids as houseplants, the situation is now much different.

If you live in even a medium-size city in the United States, you'll have access to at least a modest selection of orchids and their supplies at your local garden center or home-improvement center. Still, for a more complete offering of more unusual or desirable varieties, you may want to take a trip to an orchid grower or buy from mail order suppliers. In the appendix, I give you a list of dependable and reputable companies that offer plants and growing supplies.

I also give you contacts that you can make in order to join a national orchid society or to find your local chapter. Rubbing shoulders with other folks who share your passion for orchids is great fun.

# Chapter 15

# The Ten (or So) Easiest Orchids to Grow

*In This Chapter*

▶ Finding the orchid that's right for you

▶ Choosing an orchid that grows well where you live

T hroughout this book, I let you know about orchids that are not temperamental or especially demanding, but the orchids in this chapter are some of the most satisfying to grow because of their high performance and low maintenance.

For more specific cultural information on these orchids and others, see the chapters in Part III.

## Twinkle Moth Orchid (Phalaenopsis Twinkle)

There are so many excellent moth orchids around, that finding a "bad" one would be a challenge. In recent years, the breeders of moth orchids have reached a high level of perfection with these flowers, which means that the ones you buy at the discount center for $20 to $30 would have been prize winners several years ago.

The Twinkle moth orchid is not the typical large white, pink, or striped variety. It represents a somewhat newer direction for moth orchids — the multifloral type that has many smaller flowers, up to about 2 inches (5 cm) in size, on a very compact plant. The larger moth orchids are gorgeous and elegant but take up quite a bit of room, so if you're looking for something more compact, check out this multifloral type.

You don't need to get this specific variety of moth orchid. Just find one that's listed as a multifloral type (also sometimes referred to as "sweetheart" phalaenopsis).

# Lady of the Night (Brassavola nodosa)

This native of Mexico got its common name from its glorious freesia evening scent. It grows best in strong light with warm temperatures and will reward you with single or clusters of white spidery flowers up to 6 inches (15 cm) across, which can appear a few times a year.

Lady of the Night is a very compact-growing orchid, with tubular leaves. It's usually not more than a foot tall and grows in clumps. It will perform best if it isn't divided and is allowed to grow into a nice large plant.

# Maudiae Lady's Slipper Orchid (Paphiopedilum Maudiae)

Most Asian lady's slipper orchids, as a group, are among the easiest of orchids to grow, but this type stands out as especially undemanding. The flowers are exotic and either have dramatic burgundy markings or are elegantly colored in green and white (see the color section of photographs for an example).

Even when this plant is not in flower, its foliage is stunning with its marbled pattern against a dark green base. These orchids do well in modest light and normal room temperatures. They only grow about 8 to 10 inches (20.3 to 25.4 cm) tall, so they fit easily on any windowsill or under lights. To see these plants really shine, let them get larger and develop multiple growths, which won't take long because they're so robust.

# Cockleshell Orchid (Epidendrum cochleatum)

This is one of the most resilient of orchids — it seems to keep blooming despite less-than-ideal conditions. One of the orchids naturally found in Florida, this Cockleshell orchid has fascinating flowers that appear to look upside-down. The "cockleshell" part of the flower is striped with purple veins against a light green background, and the rest of the flower consists of segments that are narrow, green, and somewhat spidery looking. After this orchid is established, it will bloom multiple times in a row, so it can have flowers for six months or longer. It grows well under lights or on a bright windowsill.

# Sharry Baby Oncidium (Oncidium 'Sharry Baby')

This is thought to be the single most popular orchid in the world! And it's not difficult to see why. It has a great deal to offer any orchid lover.

Sharry Baby blooms dependably — usually around Christmastime — and when it does, you're treated to a flurry of many ½-inch (1.5-cm) flowers that are yellow overlaid with burgundy covering a spike of up to 30 inches (75 cm). What a show!

And the piece de resistance is that the flowers have the delicious fragrance of chocolate and vanilla!

Because this orchid can get tall, place it near a sunny window that has some headroom. Many different color forms of this wildly popular orchid are available.

# Bird-Beak Orchid (Oncidium ornithorhynchum)

Everyone has room for this Mexican beauty. Its dainty 1-inch (2.5-cm) lavender-pink flowers with bright yellow centers and white lips are borne in profusion (up to 100 on a mature plant), on thin pendulous sprays.

Because this plant only grows 6 to 8 inches tall (15 to 20 cm), it can fit on any windowsill or under lights. It will sometimes bloom more than once a year — usually in the spring, occasionally in the fall — and has a scent that reminds me of a fresh morning's air.

# Mari's Song (Laeliocattleya 'Mari's Song')

This variety belongs to a category of plants called *minicatts* (miniature cattleyas). They all take up much less space than the standard sized cattleya and many of them bloom more than once a year. This particular variety of minicatt is popular because it's easy to grow, compact, has gaily tricolored, 4½-inch (11-cm) flowers, and is very fragrant.

# Fan-Shape Orchid (Cochleanthes amazonica)

I love this orchid. It has handsome glossy green foliage. Mine frequently blooms twice or more a year with 2-inch (5-cm) snow-white flowers that are veined in dark purple and smell like sweet candy. Other cochleanthes, like *Cochleanthes discolor*, and hybrids *Cochleanthes* 'Moliere' and *Cochleanthes* 'Amazing' are also good choices. All of them have similar cultural requirements as moth orchids and are just as undemanding.

# Pansy Orchid (Miltoniopsis santanei)

Pansy orchids have a reputation for being a bit finicky. Although this may be true for some of the ones from cooler climates, I have found this species to be a wonderful exception. It's from a warmer climate so adapts very well to home culture. It has a relatively small stature, usually growing only 6 to 8 inches (15 to 20 cm) tall and sports flat, 2-inch (5-cm), white, pansy-shaped flowers with a flare of bright yellow on the top of the lip. It has a delightful rose fragrance.

To keep this orchid happy, grow it in moderate light and keep its potting material damp.

# Chapter 16

# The Ten Most Common Ways Orchids Are Killed

Sooner or later, everyone loses a few orchids to the Grim Reaper, but some causes of death take more orchid lives than they should. Being on the lookout to prevent these problems will save many of your orchids.

## Overwatering

Overwatering is the big killer of orchids. Some people just can't help themselves. Watering is so much fun and you feel like you're doing something to help your orchids when you're watering them.

When orchids die from overwatering, it isn't really the result of too much water. It's actually caused by too little air. There's just so much open space in any potting material, and water naturally displaces air, so if you apply it too often, there's no room for air. And your orchid needs air for healthy root growth. If it doesn't get enough air, the roots rot and die.

See Chapter 6 for tips on how to properly water your orchids and an emergency treatment to try if any of your overwatered orchids start going downhill.

## Underwatering

Ironically, just as overwatering is a big killer, so is underwatering. In this case, the lack of water leads to root damage by dehydration (see Chapter 6 for more details). Because orchid potting material drains much more rapidly and tends to hold less moisture than materials commonly used for other plants, some people tend to underwater. Also, remember that the fresh potting material dries out much more quickly than older potting material does.

Be sure to premoisten the orchid potting material before you use it. This will make it more water-retentive. Check out Chapter 7 for orchid potting tips and information.

# Too Much Light or Heat

Light and heat are related to one another. Frequently, excessive light leads to high temperatures. When the orchids receive too much light, the heat starts to build up inside the leaf. Think of the orchid leaf's skin being like a plastic bag with very small holes in it. Inside of this plastic bag is the interior of the leaf. When excessive heat gets trapped inside the leaf, it literally cooks and destroys the leaf plant tissue. Large black circular dead spots form, or in extreme cases, the entire orchid collapses. After this damage is done, you can't do anything about it.

When the orchid is in full illumination, feel the leaf surface with your hand. If it's hot to the touch, move the orchid to where it gets less light. See Chapter 5 for more information on light and temperature requirements for orchids.

# Leaving Orchid Foliage Wet Overnight

Leaving orchid foliage wet overnight is asking for trouble in the form of leaf spots and crown rot disease. (The *crown* is the growing point of the orchid.) Water your orchids in the morning or early afternoon, so the leaves have plenty of time to dry before nightfall.

If you can catch these diseases early, you may be able to save the orchid. But after the disease (which shows up as soft, mushy tissue, that eventually turns black) gets to the growing point of the plant, it's good-bye for your orchid.

For more information on orchid diseases and their control, see Chapter 9.

# Too Much Fertilizer

Fertilizers are salts, and salts, in concentrated form, are types of *herbicides* (plant poisons). Applying too much fertilizer will dehydrate the orchid roots. Signs of too much fertilizer are black root tips or black or brown leaf tips. So, when you fertilize, be careful not to apply more than the recommended dosage, and only use a fertilizer when the plant is actively growing and when the growing media is damp.

For more information on fertilizing orchids, see Chapter 6.

# Improper Use of Pesticides

When pesticides are used properly, they're safe for both you and your plants. However, if they're applied at too high of a concentration or applied when the plants are dry or the air temperature is too high, severe damage to the orchid plant can result.

Also, many pesticides are dissolved and mixed in with a type of oil, which in and of itself can cause leaf damage, especially if the material is applied in bright, hot sunlight.

So use care with these materials and always read the label before applying the chemical. See Chapter 9 to see which pesticides are safest and most effective to use.

# Insects

Catching insect problems in the early stages is very important. If you realize that your orchid is completely covered with an insect like scale or mealybugs, getting rid of all of them is very difficult.

Sometimes trashing this plant for the sake of others in your collection is the best approach; you don't want to expose your other plants to these critters. For more information on common orchid pests and their control, check out Chapter 9.

# Purchase of Sick Plants

Some orchid growers are Florence Nightingale types who feel it's their mission to save an orchid that looks sick. So they buy it, usually at a great discount. In most cases, these orchid lovers don't get a "deal" at all.

I highly recommend you resist the temptation to buy an unhealthy orchid and try to nurse it back to health. If an orchid is in poor condition and the leaves are wilting or shriveled, it's usually on an unstoppable death spiral and the likelihood of your bringing it back to robustness is slim to none.

# Poor Water Quality

In certain parts of the country, notably in the West, some local water has a high salt content, which can be very damaging to orchids. It can cause the same problems as overfertilizing (see "Too Much Fertilizer," earlier in this chapter).

If you have any doubts about the quality of your water, have a water test done by a company that tests water for drinking quality. Also, don't use water that has been treated with a water softener on your orchids. It usually contains a high amount of salt.

For more information on water quality, see Chapter 6.

# Inadequate Ventilation

Orchids don't appreciate stale air. When air isn't circulated, fungi and bacterial diseases flourish. Moving air also evaporates moisture on leaves (moisture on leaves is another cause for disease problems). So make your orchid happy and invest in an overhead ceiling fan or oscillating fan to keep the air gently moving. It will make a great difference in the health of your orchids. For more on ventilation, see Chapter 5.

# Chapter 17

# The Ten Most Frequently Asked Questions about Orchids

. . . . . . . . . . . . . . . . . . . . . . . . . . . . . . . . . . . . . . .

### In This Chapter

▶ Figuring out whether orchids are right for you

▶ Easing your mind with the orchid answers you need

. . . . . . . . . . . . . . . . . . . . . . . . . . . . . . . . . . . . . . .

This entire book covers everything you need to know about orchids, but in this chapter, I answer some of the most common questions that beginning orchid growers have.

## Are Orchids Difficult to Grow?

Orchids aren't difficult to grow — they just have particular require-ments that are somewhat different from many other houseplants you may be familiar with. Thanks to modern orchid breeding, many of the orchids that are available for beginning orchid lovers are vig-orous growers that are adaptable to a wide range of growing situa-tions, and that bloom easily and frequently.

Selecting the right orchid for your conditions is one of the keys to success. See Chapter 2 to help you choose which one will do well for you.

## Why Should 1 Grow Orchids?

Many expert and amateur gardeners consider orchids to be the most beautiful and exotic members of the plant family. Orchids are a huge group of plants with diverse cultural requirements. This means that, no matter where you live, you can find a group of orchids that will suit your growing area. Also, because the flower forms, fragrances, and colors are so diverse, you can find an orchid to satisfy your taste.

Growing orchids is more than merely cultivating plants. You'll be joining a fraternity of avid (if not fanatical) orchid people who share your interests. Soon you may become a member of an orchid society (see the appendix), and you may visit various orchid growers and attend orchid shows. You'll form new friendships with others who share your passion. It's said that, after you're bitten by the orchid bug, there is no known cure. But what a wonderful affliction!

# Do I Need a Greenhouse to Grow Orchids?

Absolutely not! Years ago, orchids were reserved for wealthy people who could afford elaborate greenhouses with an attending staff of professional horticulturists. Although a few of these places are still around today, most people now grow orchids on windowsills and under florescent lights. I've grown most of my orchids that way and have been pleased to produce plants and flowers that look as good as those grown in a greenhouse. So, don't despair: If you have a sunny window or a place to set up some lights, you, too, can grow these beauties.

# Are Orchids Expensive?

They don't need to be. Sure, if you're bound and determined, you can spend thousands of dollars on mature, awarded plants. But today you can buy blooming-size, fine-quality, healthy beginner orchids ranging in price from $20 to $30. This is less than the price of a flower arrangement from the florist, and an orchid's flowers will usually last much longer. After the orchid is finished flowering, you still have a plant ready to bloom with even more flowers every year. They're really quite the floral bargain.

# How Long and How Often Will Orchids Bloom?

This varies, depending on the type of orchid. A few orchids only bloom a couple of days, but most will have flowers that last anywhere from a few weeks to a couple of months. Some with the longest lasting flowers are the slipper and moth orchids. Many orchids bloom once a year, while others can bloom two or three times a year.

# What Makes an Orchid an Orchid?

When many people see orchids, they can't imagine what so many diverse plants have in common that makes them all orchids. They look so different! You have to closely examine the flower for the answers. If you study the inner part of the flower, you'll see a club-like structure that houses the male and female flower parts *(stamens* and *pistils)* called the *column.* All orchids have this unique structure. Most also have a large and conspicuous center petal called a *lip.*

For more information about how orchid plants and their flowers are distinctive, see Chapter 1.

# Are Orchids Fragrant?

Not all orchids are fragrant, but many are. A wonderful aspect of orchid fragrance is their range of scents. Some smell like other flowers (carnations, jasmine, gardenia, rose), while others have the scents of spices and foods (vanilla, citrus, cloves, chocolate, coconut, licorice, honey, cinnamon, grapes).

Some orchids even reek! These are orchids that are pollinated by flies and other insects attracted to *carrion* (rotted meat). Fortunately, very few orchids fall in this category and they're easy to pick out when selecting orchids from a grower's greenhouse.

See the Cheat Sheet in the front of the book for a list of some wonderfully fragrant orchids. And watch for the Fragrance icon throughout this book to find orchids that have distinctive scents.

# Where Can I See the Best Collections of Orchids?

Many public gardens display a sampling of these plants because they put on such a show. For outstanding exhibits of orchids, check out the following:

- ✔ **Longwood Gardens,** Route 1, P.O. Box 501, Kennett Square, PA 19348-0501; phone: 610-388-1000; Web: www.longwood gardens.org.

- ✔ **Missouri Botanical Garden,** 4344 Shaw Blvd., St. Louis, MO 63110; phone: 800-642-8842 (toll-free) or 314-577-9400; Web: www.mobot.org.

- ✔ **New York Botanical Garden,** Bronx River Parkway and Fordham Road, Bronx, NY 10458-5126; phone: 718-817-8700; Web: www.nybg.org.

- ✔ **The American Orchid Society Visitor's Center and Botanical Garden,** 16700 AOS Lane, Delray Beach, FL 33446; phone: 561-404-2045; Web: http://orchidweb.org.

- ✔ **Atlanta Botanical Garden,** 1345 Piedmont Ave. NE, Atlanta, GA 30309; phone: 404-876-5859; Web site: www.atlanta botanicalgarden.org.

- ✔ **Los Angeles County Arboretum & Botanic Garden,** 301 N. Baldwin Ave., Arcadia, CA 91007; phone: 626-821-3222; Web: www.arboretum.org.

- ✔ **San Diego Zoo,** 2920 Zoo Drive, San Diego, CA 92101; phone: 619-234-3153; Web: www.sandiegozoo.org.

To search out others in your area, see the list of orchid public-display gardens on the American Orchid Society's Web site (http://orchidweb.org/gardens.html).

Many commercial growers also have fine displays of orchids at their greenhouses. Regional orchid shows are held yearly in almost every major city in the United States; they're great places to see orchids.

# Are Any Orchids Hardy?

Most orchids (and all the ones described in this book) are from tropical or semitropical areas and are intended to be grown as indoor houseplants in most of the United States. In warmer states, like parts of California, Texas, and Florida, some of these orchids can be grown outdoors with winter protection.

There are, however, other native orchids that can only grow well in very northern climates. The various lady's slipper orchids are the ones most admired in this group. In fact, one of these, the Spotted Lady's Slipper, is only found in the Yukon and Alaska!

# Are Orchids Parasites?

Orchids are not parasites. Some people, who have seen orchids growing in the wild in the tropics, have noticed that many of them are attached to the limbs and trunks of trees, so they make the conclusion that, like mistletoe, orchids are parasites. Parasites, by definition, get their food at the expense of their host plants. This is not the case with orchids. They're merely using the trees or shrubs as places to grow. Orchids are often found in the crotches of the limbs where water and nutrients from roosting birds naturally accumulate. Orchids have roots that can absorb these nutrients, and the high perches in the trees afford them plenty of moist air circulation, natural rainfall, and exposure to sunlight.

# Chapter 18

# The Ten Most Common Reasons Why Orchids Don't Bloom

• • • • • • • • • • • • • • • • • • • • • • • • • • • • • • • • • • • •

### In This Chapter

▶ Knowing how to keep your orchids blooming

▶ Giving your orchids what they need

• • • • • • • • • • • • • • • • • • • • • • • • • • • • • • • • • • • •

*N*othing is more frustrating than having your orchid plants look good and healthy but still not bloom. This is a common problem that can be easily remedied, and in this chapter, I show you how.

## Not Enough Difference between Day and Night Temperatures

The most common reason that orchids don't bloom indoors is that the environment doesn't have enough of a change in temperature between day and night. In orchids' natural habitats, evening temperatures are at least 10°F to 15°F lower than the daytime temperatures. This temperature difference triggers the orchids to start developing flowers. In many home environments, the temperature doesn't vary much between day and night.

 Get yourself a maximum-minimum thermometer (see Chapter 3) and place it in your growing room. This thermometer will tell you if you need to move the plant somewhere cooler in the evening, like closer to the window.

If you summer your orchids outdoors during the summer (see Chapter 5), you'll easily be able to provide this temperature difference. The temperature in my orchid summering area outdoors drops in the evening at least 15°F and sometimes 20°F or more during late summer and early fall.

# Too Moist during the Winter

Several orchids, like some of the dendrobiums, require a very dry period, up to several weeks, during the winter, when very little water should be given to the plants. This mimics their native habitat, in which their winters are dry. This dry period triggers flower buds to form. Then when watering or natural rainfall begins in the spring, the buds are ready to swell and produce flowers.

# Too Little Light

If the leaves of your orchids are very dark green, the new growth is longer or "stretched" compared to the older growth, and the leaves on the stems are farther and farther apart, these are signs that your orchid is not receiving enough light. Orchids will survive in this lower light, but they won't bloom. They need more energy from light in order to produce flowers.

If your orchid is displaying these symptoms, gradually increase its exposure to light by placing it in a brighter window or moving it closer to florescent lights. See Chapter 5 for more information on orchid light requirements and how to meet your orchid's needs.

# Excessively High or Low Temperatures

Excessively high or low temperatures can either prevent buds from forming or can cause the buds that are starting to develop to shrivel and fall off. Unfortunately, flower buds are very vulnerable to any forms of environmental stress, and they react to this stress by falling, shrinking, and drying up before they open.

When orchids are shipped in cold weather, the low temperatures that they experience in transit can cause them to drop their buds. When you buy orchids during the winter that have been shipped to the store, wait until they've been in the store for a day or so to see if the buds have been affected by their trip.

# Not Using a Fertilizer or Using One with Too Much Nitrogen

Most orchids have relatively low nutrient needs, but, because they're usually grown in bark mixes that have few nutrients, some type of fertilizer is usually necessary to provide their basic requirements.

Applying fertilizers with too much nitrogen can also cause poor or no blooming. High-nitrogen fertilizers can stimulate lush leaf growth at the expense of flowers. See Chapter 6 for more-specific orchid fertilizing guidelines.

# Immature Plants

If you purchase an orchid that hasn't bloomed, it may not yet have reached its mature size. The amount of time it takes for an orchid to mature varies a great deal depending on the type of orchid. For instance, moth orchids are very fast to mature, while some of the others may take years. Plants that have not yet bloomed are usually sold as seedlings (which can take several years to reach maturity), as NFS (*near flowering size,* which usually bloom within a year), or as FS (*flowering size,* which means they've reached mature size and will usually bloom within several months).

# Too Low Humidity

If the air is too dry when the buds are forming, they'll sometimes dry up before they open. To prevent this from happening to your orchids, keep the humidly in your growing area at 60 percent or greater.

See Chapter 5 for tips on how to easily raise the humidity around your orchids.

# Disease, Insects, or Mice

Orchid buds that are ravaged by insect pests or attacked by diseases will either shrivel in place or, when they open, be deformed. Follow the disease and insect prevention and control methods outlined in Chapter 9.

Some chemical pesticide sprays that you may use on insects and disease can cause damage to the flower buds, so be careful to spray-test a few buds at first before you apply the material to the entire plant. If possible, wash the bugs off with warm water instead of applying chemical sprays to the buds.

Mice also have the annoying habit of waiting until the flower buds are plump and just ready to open before they decide to make a meal of them. If your flower buds just disappear one night, suspect mice as the likely culprits.

# Not Enough Water

When flower buds are starting to swell, their cells are filling up with water like a balloon. If sufficient water is not available to the developing buds when all this is happening, they won't fully develop and instead will shrivel and never recover.

Cold water can also have the effect of causing the buds to drop off before the flowers open. To prevent this, use water that is room temperature or slightly warmer.

# Recently Transplanted and Divided

When an orchid is transplanted, roots are frequently damaged, which causes stress to the plant by reducing the roots' ability to effectively supply water to the buds.

Interestingly, after the flower is fully formed and open, transplanting and or dividing rarely does much harm. In fact, some people routinely transplant their orchids when they're in flower, although I think you're better off waiting until right after they flower to transplant them. For more information on transplanting and dividing, see Chapter 7.

# Appendix

# Resources

• • • • • • • • • • • • • • • • • • • • • • • • • • • • • • • • • • • • • • •

## *Plant Suppliers*

You may be fortunate enough to live close to an orchid grower, but if you don't or if you just want the convenience of buying by mail, you may want to try out some of the suppliers in this section. All these folks are people who specialize in orchids. Some have print catalogs; all have Web sites. For more information on how to find orchid suppliers, check out Chapter 2.

**Andy's Orchids,** 734 Oceanview Ave., Encinitas, CA 92024; Phone: 888-514-2639; Fax: 888-632-8991; E-mail: info@andysorchids.com; Web site: www.andysorchids.com. This company grows over 3,000 species of orchids. Most of them are mounted on pieces of wood. The Web site has a very effective search engine you can use to look for the types of orchids you want.

**AnTec Laboratory,** P.O. Box 65, 362 West Candor Rd., Candor, NY 13743; Phone: 607-659-3330; Fax: 607-659-4203; E-mail: antec@lady slipper.com; Web site: www.ladyslipper.com. This is a grower and breeder who specializes in slipper orchids. Their Web site is rich with articles and photos of slipper orchids.

**Big Leaf Orchids,** 4932 Longwood Court, Irving, TX 75038; Phone: 972-659-1406; Fax: 972-659-1438; E-mail: phal@bigleaforchids. com; Web site: www.bigleaforchids.com. Peter Lin, the owner of this small, backyard company, is a lover of phalaenopsis. Check out the Web site for some fine-quality clones and crosses. His site hosts a phalaenopsis forum that is highly informative.

**C & C Orchids,** P.O. Box 3685, Olathe, Kansas 66063; Phone: 913-338-4127; Fax: 913-338-4127; E-mail: contact@cncorchids. com; Web site: www.cncorchids.com. Taiwan has become the world's leader in phalaenopsis breeding. This company offers high-quality mature cloned plants from Taiwan at reasonable prices. Web catalog only.

**Cal-Orchid,** 1251 Orchid Dr., Santa Barbara, CA 93111; Phone: 805-967-1312; Fax: 805-967-6882; E-mail: info@calorchid.com; Web site: www.calorchid.com. Lauris and James Rose are the owners, and they've been in the orchid business since 1970. They offer a fine selection of orchids, many of which are ideal for beginners. Web catalog only.

**Carter and Holmes Orchids,** 629 Mendelhall Rd., P.O. Box 668, Newberry, SC 29108; Phone: 803-276-0579; Fax: 803-276-0588; E-mail: orchids@carterandholmes.com; Web site: www.carterandholmes.com. Mac Holmes is the third-generation owner of this well-respected orchid nursery that offers a large range of orchids at reasonable prices.

**Countryside Orchids,** P.O. Box 958, Corrales, NM 87048; Phone: 505-263-6888; Fax: 505-792-9807; E-mail: billschn@aol.com; Web site: http://members.aol.com/CSOrchids/. This company has an absolutely mind-boggling offering of orchids. Their online catalog is highly informative. An amazing resource!

**Everglades Orchids,** 1101 Tabit Rd., Belle Glade, FL 33430; Phone: 561-996-9600; E-mail: milton@evergladesorchids.com; Web site: www.evergladesorchids.com. This company specializes in orchids in the oncidium hybrids and in cymbidiums.

**Gold Country Orchids,** 390 Big Ben Rd., Lincoln CA 95648; Phone: 916-645-8600; Fax: 916-645-7076; E-mail: gcorchids@aol.com; Web site: www.goldcountryorchids.com. Alan Koch, the owner of this nursery, is one of the few orchid breeders who is putting a lot of effort into producing compact and miniature cattleyas. Visit the Web site for online ordering.

**Ha'iku Maui Orchids, Inc.,** 2612 Pololei Place, Ha'iku, HI 96708; Phone: 808-573-1130; Fax: 808-572-7015; E-mail: haikumaui.orchids@verizon.net; Web site: www.haikumauiorchids.com. Norman Mizuno, the president of this company, is from New York, where he grew prize-winning orchids under lights. He specializes in orchids and selected forms that are easy to grow. The company makes special efforts to grow their plants under lower light conditions, so the plants will adapt well to growers on the mainland.

**Hoosier Orchid Company,** 8440 West 82nd St., Indianapolis, IN 46278; Phone: 888-291-6269; Fax: 317-291-8949; E-mail: orchids@hoosierorchid.com; Web site: www.hoosierorchid.com. This company offers an impressive array of orchid species.

**I. N. Komoda Orchids,** P.O. Box 576, Makawao, HI 96768; Phone/Fax: 808-572-0756; E-mail: orchidhi@maui.net; Web site: http://orchidmall.com/komoda/. Ivan Komoda, the owner, specializes and primarily breeds gorgeous miltoniopsis.

**J & L Orchids,** 20 Sherwood Rd., Easton, CT 06612; Phone: 203-261-3772; Fax: 203-261-8730; E-mail: jlorchid@snet.net; Web site: www.jandlorchids.com. A miniature-orchid lover's paradise. The highly knowledgeable owners, Cordelia Head, Marguerite Webb, and Lucinda Winn, know their orchids. They have print and online catalogs.

**Krull-Smith,** 2815 West Ponkan Rd., Apopkam, FL 32712; Phone: 407-886-4134; Fax: 407-886-0438; E-mail: sales@krullsmith.com; Web site: www.krullsmith.com. A somewhat limited selection, but what they have is first class.

**Lauray of Salisbury,** 432 Undermountain Rd., Route 41, Salisbury, CT 06068; Phone: 860-435-2263; E-mail: jbecker@mohawk.net; Web site: www.lauray.com. Judy Becker is the owner and operator of this business. She is an American Orchid Society judge, which means she's highly knowledgeable about orchids. Her company offers a broad range of orchid species and hybrids, as well as some suitable orchid companions like begonias, gesnerias, and succulents.

**Norman's Orchids,** 11039 Monte Vista Ave., Montclair, CA 91763; Phone: 909-627-9515; Fax: 909-627-3889; E-mail: support@orchids.com; Web site: www.orchids.com. This company has one of most useful and easiest sites for purchasing orchids online that I've ever experienced. You can search by various requirements — light needs, color of flower, size of plant, fragrance — to come up with the orchids that fit your needs. Then you can keep these orchids stored in your wish list until you're ready to purchase. Web catalog only.

**Oak Hill Gardens,** 37W550 Binnie Rd., P. O. Box 25, Dundee, IL 60118; Phone: 847-428-8500; Fax: 847-428-8527; E-mail: oakhillgardens@sprintmail.com; Web site: www.oakhillgardens.com. Oak Hill offers a fine selection of orchids at very reasonable prices.

**Parkside Orchid Nursery,** 2503 Mountainview Dr. (Route 563), Ottsville, PA 18942; Phone: 610-847-8039; E-mail: parkside@ptd.net; Web site: www.parksideorchids.com. This orchid nursery specialist has myriad types of orchids and their Web site has listings of all their plants in bud, so you won't have to wait long to see results!

**Phoenix Orchids,** 2807 West Villa Rita Dr., Phoenix, AZ 85053; Phone: 602-938-3741; E-mail: phxorchids@msn.com; Web site: www.phoenixorchids.com. Eric Goo, the owner of Phoenix Orchids, is a breeder of phalaenopsis. He has bred and offers some of the newest and best phalaenopsis with his primary focus being the reds and yellows. Web catalog only.

**Piping Rock Orchids,** 2270 Cook Rd., Galway, NY 12074; Phone/Fax: 518-882-9002; E-mail: PipingRock@aol.com; Web site: www.pipingrockorchids.com. The owner, Glen Decker, is highly regarded for the high-quality slipper orchids he produces. They have print and online catalogs.

**Porter's Orchids,** 10868 Royston Rd., Grand Ledge, MI 48837; Phone: 888-622-7643; Fax: 517-622-4188; E-mail: orchidsuzi@aol.com; Web site: www.portersorchids.com. This company specializes in orchids that are easy to grow and bloom and are well-suited to home culture. They offer a broad range of hybrids and species.

**R. F. Orchids,** 28100 SW 182nd Ave., Homestead, FL 33030; Phone: 305-245-4570; Fax: 305-247-6568; E-mail: rforchids@aol.com; Web site: www.rforchids.com. This firm is one of the world leaders in the breeding and growing of vandas, ascocendas, and their relatives. Some of their plants will not be suitable for small spaces and for parts of the country with low light, but others, such as the dwarf varieties, are great choices.

**Santa Barbara Orchid Estate,** 1250 Orchid Dr., Santa Barbara, CA 93111; Phone: 805-967-1284; Fax 805-683-3405; E-mail: sboe@sborchid.com; Web site: www.sborchid.com. This company offers many different orchids but specializes in those that will grow well outdoors in mild climates.

# Growing Supplies

Some basic growing containers and potting materials are sometimes available at your local home center or box store, but if you want a much larger selection of all supplies related to orchids, try these mail-order suppliers. If you plan to purchase heavy potting materials, you'll save quite a bit of postage if you buy from the supplier closest to you geographically.

**Calwest Orchid Supplies,** 11614 Sterling Ave., Riverside, CA 92503; Phone: 800-301-9009; Fax: 951-351-1880; E-mail: cwtropical@1stconnect.com; Web site: www.calwestorchidsupplies.com. A well-rounded selection of orchid supplies.

**Charley's Greenhouse & Garden,** 17979 State Route 536, Mount Vernon, WA 98273; Phone: 800-322-4707; Fax: 800-233-3078; E-mail: productsupport@charleysgreenhouse.com; Web site: www.charleysgreenhouse.com. Offers many orchid supplies including hobby greenhouses and artificial light setups that are ideal for orchid growing.

**Indoor Gardening Supplies (IGS),** P.O. Box 527, Dexter, MI 48130; Phone: 800-823-5740; Fax: 866-823-4978; E-mail: IGS@indoorgardensupplies.com; Web site: www.indoorgardensupplies.com. Offers a full line of light gardening supplies suited for orchid growing.

**Kelley's Korner Orchid Supplies,** P. O. Box 6, Kittery, ME 03904; Phone: 207-439-0922; Fax: 207-439-8202; E-mail: info@kkorchid.com; Web site: www.kkorchid.com. Carries a broad range of potting supplies, pots, equipment, tools, fertilizers, and pest controls. Print and Web catalog.

**OFE International,** P.O. Box 161081, Miami, FL 33116; Phone: 305-253-7080; Fax: 305-251-8285; E-mail: sales@ofe-intl.com; Web site: www.ofe-intl.com. Their motto — "Everything for growing orchids under one roof" — says it all. They have a huge selection and the online ordering is very easy to use. Print and Web catalog.

**Roberts Flower Supply,** 12390 Root Rd., Columbia Station, OH 44028; Phone: 440-236-5571; E-mail: rfs@orchidmix.com; Web site: www.orchidmix.com. A wide offering of orchid potting materials. They also sell hardy slipper orchids (cypripedium).

**US Orchid Supplies,** 1621 South Rose Ave., Oxnard, CA 93033; Phone: 805-247-0086; Fax: 805-247-0087; E-mail: sales@usorchidsupplies.com; Web site: www.usorchidsupplies.com. This company sells potting supplies, fertilizers, and pest controls.

# Orchid Societies

Various societies specialize in specific kinds of orchids, but the ones I list here are among the biggest and most established.

**The American Orchid Society,** 16700 AOS Lane, Delray Beach, FL 33446; Phone: 561-404-2000; Fax: 561-404-2100; E-mail: TheAOS@aos.org; Web site: www.aos.org. This is simply a fabulous orchid society! I've been a member for over 30 years. Their monthly publication, *Orchids,* is unparalleled in the orchid world and is filled with sumptuous color photos and articles that are of interest to beginners as well as aficionados. Their Web site is full of information, including cultural sheets, the most complete orchid bookstore around, an extensive list of orchid suppliers throughout the United States and the world, a calendar of orchid events, their own high-quality booklets, a discussion forum, and links to all the affiliated societies through the United States (and the world). If you're bitten by the orchid bug, you owe it to yourself to join this fine organization.

**International Phalaenopsis Alliance,** 1540 Anne Dr., West Chester, PA 19380; Phone: 610-431-7633; E-mail: mcrna2go@aol.com; Web site: www.phal.org. For you moth orchid lovers, their superb, full-color journal, *Phalaenopsis,* is a must and is the primary benefit of joining this organization. It also sponsors national and regional orchid workshops.

**Orchid Digest,** Membership, P.O. Box 10360, Canoga Park, CA 91309; Fax: 323-464-0915; E-mail: membership@orchiddigest.org; Web site: www.orchiddigest.org. This group produces an excellent magazine, *Orchid Digest,* published quarterly. It is an elegant and highly informational publication that I can't imagine being without.

**Royal Horticultural Society,** 80 Vincent Square, London, SW1P 2PE, United Kingdom; Phone: +44 020 7834 4333; E-mail: info@rhs.org.uk; Web site: www.rhs.org.uk. This is the oldest orchid society in the world and so is its periodical, *The Orchid Review. The Orchid Review,* published six times a year, is a bit more esoteric than *Orchids* and *Orchid Digest,* but if you just can't get enough information about orchids, this is another one to add to your list. To subscribe to *The Orchid Review,* go to the RHS Web site and click on Publications, then follow the Orchid Review link, or e-mail orchidreview@rhs.org.uk.

# Index

# • *M* •

# Notes

# Notes

## BUSINESS, CAREERS & PERSONAL FINANCE

0-7645-5307-0    0-7645-5331-3 *†

**Also available:**

- ✓ Accounting For Dummies †
  0-7645-5314-3
- ✓ Business Plans Kit For Dummies †
  0-7645-5365-8
- ✓ Cover Letters For Dummies
  0-7645-5224-4
- ✓ Frugal Living For Dummies
  0-7645-5403-4
- ✓ Leadership For Dummies
  0-7645-5176-0
- ✓ Managing For Dummies
  0-7645-1771-6

- ✓ Marketing For Dummies
  0-7645-5600-2
- ✓ Personal Finance For Dummies *
  0-7645-2590-5
- ✓ Project Management
  For Dummies
  0-7645-5283-X
- ✓ Resumes For Dummies †
  0-7645-5471-9
- ✓ Selling For Dummies
  0-7645-5363-1
- ✓ Small Business Kit For Dummies *†
  0-7645-5093-4

## HOME & BUSINESS COMPUTER BASICS

0-7645-4074-2    0-7645-3758-X

**Also available:**

- ✓ ACT! 6 For Dummies
  0-7645-2645-6
- ✓ iLife '04 All-in-One Desk Reference
  For Dummies
  0-7645-7347-0
- ✓ iPAQ For Dummies
  0-7645-6769-1
- ✓ Mac OS X Panther Timesaving
  Techniques For Dummies
  0-7645-5812-9
- ✓ Macs For Dummies
  0-7645-5656-8
- ✓ Microsoft Money 2004 For Dummies
  0-7645-4195-1

- ✓ Office 2003 All-in-One Desk
  Reference For Dummies
  0-7645-3883-7
- ✓ Outlook 2003 For Dummies
  0-7645-3759-8
- ✓ PCs For Dummies
  0-7645-4074-2
- ✓ TiVo For Dummies
  0-7645-6923-6
- ✓ Upgrading and Fixing PCs
  For Dummies
  0-7645-1665-5
- ✓ Windows XP Timesaving
  Techniques For Dummies
  0-7645-3748-2

## FOOD, HOME, GARDEN, HOBBIES, MUSIC & PETS

0-7645-5295-3    0-7645-5232-5

**Also available:**

- ✓ Bass Guitar For Dummies
  0-7645-2487-9
- ✓ Diabetes Cookbook For Dummies
  0-7645-5230-9
- ✓ Gardening For Dummies *
  0-7645-5130-2
- ✓ Guitar For Dummies
  0-7645-5106-X
- ✓ Holiday Decorating For Dummies
  0-7645-2570-0
- ✓ Home Improvement All-in-One
  For Dummies
  0-7645-5680-0

- ✓ Knitting For Dummies
  0-7645-5395-X
- ✓ Piano For Dummies
  0-7645-5105-1
- ✓ Puppies For Dummies
  0-7645-5255-4
- ✓ Scrapbooking For Dummies
  0-7645-7208-3
- ✓ Senior Dogs For Dummies
  0-7645-5818-8
- ✓ Singing For Dummies
  0-7645-2475-5
- ✓ 30-Minute Meals For Dummies
  0-7645-2589-1

## INTERNET & DIGITAL MEDIA

0-7645-1664-7    0-7645-6924-4

**Also available:**

- ✓ 2005 Online Shopping Directory
  For Dummies
  0-7645-7495-7
- ✓ CD & DVD Recording For Dummies
  0-7645-5956-7
- ✓ eBay For Dummies
  0-7645-5654-1
- ✓ Fighting Spam For Dummies
  0-7645-5965-6
- ✓ Genealogy Online For Dummies
  0-7645-5964-8
- ✓ Google For Dummies
  0-7645-4420-9

- ✓ Home Recording For Musicians
  For Dummies
  0-7645-1634-5
- ✓ The Internet For Dummies
  0-7645-4173-0
- ✓ iPod & iTunes For Dummies
  0-7645-7772-7
- ✓ Preventing Identity Theft
  For Dummies
  0-7645-7336-5
- ✓ Pro Tools All-in-One Desk
  Reference For Dummies
  0-7645-5714-9
- ✓ Roxio Easy Media Creator
  For Dummies
  0-7645-7131-1

\* **Separate Canadian edition also available**

† **Separate U.K. edition also available**

Available wherever books are sold. For more information or to order direct: U.S. customers visit www.dummies.com or call 1-877-762-2974.
U.K. customers visit www.wileyeurope.com or call 0800 243407. Canadian customers visit www.wiley.ca or call 1-800-567-4797.

## SPORTS, FITNESS, PARENTING, RELIGION & SPIRITUALITY

0-7645-5146-9    0-7645-5418-2

**Also available:**

✓Adoption For Dummies
0-7645-5488-3

✓Basketball For Dummies
0-7645-5248-1

✓The Bible For Dummies
0-7645-5296-1

✓Buddhism For Dummies
0-7645-5359-3

✓Catholicism For Dummies
0-7645-5391-7

✓Hockey For Dummies
0-7645-5228-7

✓Judaism For Dummies
0-7645-5299-6

✓Martial Arts For Dummies
0-7645-5358-5

✓Pilates For Dummies
0-7645-5397-6

✓Religion For Dummies
0-7645-5264-3

✓Teaching Kids to Read
For Dummies
0-7645-4043-2

✓Weight Training For Dummies
0-7645-5168-X

✓Yoga For Dummies
0-7645-5117-5

## TRAVEL

0-7645-5438-7    0-7645-5453-0

**Also available:**

✓Alaska For Dummies
0-7645-1761-9

✓Arizona For Dummies
0-7645-6938-4

✓Cancún and the Yucatán
For Dummies
0-7645-2437-2

✓Cruise Vacations For Dummies
0-7645-6941-4

✓Europe For Dummies
0-7645-5456-5

✓Ireland For Dummies
0-7645-5455-7

✓Las Vegas For Dummies
0-7645-5448-4

✓London For Dummies
0-7645-4277-X

✓New York City For Dummies
0-7645-6945-7

✓Paris For Dummies
0-7645-5494-8

✓RV Vacations For Dummies
0-7645-5443-3

✓Walt Disney World & Orlando
For Dummies
0-7645-6943-0

## GRAPHICS, DESIGN & WEB DEVELOPMENT

0-7645-4345-8    0-7645-5589-8

**Also available:**

✓Adobe Acrobat 6 PDF
For Dummies
0-7645-3760-1

✓Building a Web Site For Dummies
0-7645-7144-3

✓Dreamweaver MX 2004
For Dummies
0-7645-4342-3

✓FrontPage 2003 For Dummies
0-7645-3882-9

✓HTML 4 For Dummies
0-7645-1995-6

✓Illustrator cs For Dummies
0-7645-4084-X

✓Macromedia Flash MX 2004
For Dummies
0-7645-4358-X

✓Photoshop 7 All-in-One Desk
Reference For Dummies
0-7645-1667-1

✓Photoshop cs Timesaving
Techniques For Dummies
0-7645-6782-9

✓PHP 5 For Dummies
0-7645-4166-8

✓PowerPoint 2003 For Dummies
0-7645-3908-6

✓QuarkXPress 6 For Dummies
0-7645-2593-X

## NETWORKING, SECURITY, PROGRAMMING & DATABASES

0-7645-6852-3    0-7645-5784-X

**Also available:**

✓A+ Certification For Dummies
0-7645-4187-0

✓Access 2003 All-in-One Desk
Reference For Dummies
0-7645-3988-4

✓Beginning Programming
For Dummies
0-7645-4997-9

✓C For Dummies
0-7645-7068-4

✓Firewalls For Dummies
0-7645-4048-3

✓Home Networking For Dummies
0-7645-42796

✓Network Security For Dummies
0-7645-1679-5

✓Networking For Dummies
0-7645-1677-9

✓TCP/IP For Dummies
0-7645-1760-0

✓VBA For Dummies
0-7645-3989-2

✓Wireless All In-One Desk Reference
For Dummies
0-7645-7496-5

✓Wireless Home Networking
For Dummies
0-7645-3910-8

## HEALTH & SELF-HELP

0-7645-6820-5 *†    0-7645-2566-2

**Also available:**

- Alzheimer's For Dummies
  0-7645-3899-3
- Asthma For Dummies
  0-7645-4233-8
- Controlling Cholesterol For Dummies
  0-7645-5440-9
- Depression For Dummies
  0-7645-3900-0
- Dieting For Dummies
  0-7645-4149-8
- Fertility For Dummies
  0-7645-2549-2

- Fibromyalgia For Dummies
  0-7645-5441-7
- Improving Your Memory For Dummies
  0-7645-5435-2
- Pregnancy For Dummies †
  0-7645-4483-7
- Quitting Smoking For Dummies
  0-7645-2629-4
- Relationships For Dummies
  0-7645-5384-4
- Thyroid For Dummies
  0-7645-5385-2

## EDUCATION, HISTORY, REFERENCE & TEST PREPARATION

0-7645-5194-9    0-7645-4186-2

**Also available:**

- Algebra For Dummies
  0-7645-5325-9
- British History For Dummies
  0-7645-7021-8
- Calculus For Dummies
  0-7645-2498-4
- English Grammar For Dummies
  0-7645-5322-4
- Forensics For Dummies
  0-7645-5580-4
- The GMAT For Dummies
  0-7645-5251-1
- Inglés Para Dummies
  0-7645-5427-1

- Italian For Dummies
  0-7645-5196-5
- Latin For Dummies
  0-7645-5431-X
- Lewis & Clark For Dummies
  0-7645-2545-X
- Research Papers For Dummies
  0-7645-5426-3
- The SAT I For Dummies
  0-7645-7193-1
- Science Fair Projects For Dummies
  0-7645-5460-3
- U.S. History For Dummies
  0-7645-5249-X

# Get smart @ dummies.com®

- **Find a full list of Dummies titles**
- **Look into loads of FREE on-site articles**
- **Sign up for FREE eTips e-mailed to you weekly**
- **See what other products carry the Dummies name**
- **Shop directly from the Dummies bookstore**
- **Enter to win new prizes every month!**

\* Separate Canadian edition also available
† Separate U.K. edition also available

Available wherever books are sold. For more information or to order direct: U.S. customers visit www.dummies.com or call 1-877-762-2974.
U.K. customers visit www.wileyeurope.com or call 0800 243407. Canadian customers visit www.wiley.ca or call 1-800-567-4797.